Dream
Your Life, Your Future

John Peter Wilson

PUBLISHING

Dream: Your Life, Your Future

First published in 2012 by 2QT Limited (Publishing)

The information described in this book is not intended to replace the advice of a healthcare professional. You are recommended always to seek professional guidance. The author and publisher claim no responsibility to any person or entity for any liability, loss, or damage caused or alleged to be caused directly or indirectly as a result of the application, use or interpretation of the contents in this book.

A CIP catalogue record of this book is available from the British Library

ISBN: 978-1-908098-71-9

Designed and typeset by Ian Smith
Printed and bound in China on behalf of Latitude Press Limited

Acknowledgements

To all people, organisations and countries:
Dream your dreams often, because they become your future.

Illustrations
Colin Beard, Tom Farrow, Alison Lilburn: Rotherham Imagination
Library, Jo Menezes, Ian Smith, Jenny Smith, University of Sheffield,
Nicolas Willens, Rebecca Wilson, John Peter Wilson

CONTENTS

PREFACE

It all begins with a dream. Apart from the natural world, almost everything we see originally began as a waking dream of what might be inside our head. To achieve something we must first think about it before we can translate it into action. This can involve thinking about relatively ordinary things such as what you are going to wear for the day, and making a cup of tea or coffee. On a larger and more important scale it can involve areas such as planning a career, identifying personal characteristics in a desirable partner, designing a home, planning a business etc. in the future.

But the future has yet to happen and so we have to use our imagination to explore what might happen. And the more we develop this personal capacity to dream about the future the greater potential there is that it will happen. This is not about a fantasy land, instead it is a practical approach in which we take personal responsibility for our future and anticipate the consequences of our potential actions.

This book presents new and original ideas which are beginning to have a major impact on those who apply them in constructive ways. It is based upon extensive scientific research which is linked to psychology and the exciting area of cognitive science – the study of the brain. Don't worry! This book will not lose you in complicated terminology, instead, it will provide you with simple guidelines and practical solutions which can make your life more successful.

By putting into practice the foundations described in this book you can influence your own future by creating your own luck; improving your health; changing your perceptions; increasing your physical and mental strength; changing the way you think; and enabling you to avoid short-term temptations and giving you a long term perspective to build a successful future. It can also inspire you to achieve things which you may never have thought possible.

In this book we are going to look at why dreaming is so important to our wellbeing and existence; read about some dreamers and the magnificent things they have achieved; and practice the art of dreaming so that we too can live our dreams. Moreover, our dreams need not be just about ourselves but can include our family, friends, business, community, country, and our planet.

1

WHY DO PEOPLE DAYDREAM?

"Dream lofty dreams, and as you dream, so shall you become. Your vision is the promise of what you shall one day be; your ideal is the prophecy of what you shall at last unveil."
JAMES ALLEN (1864 -1912) ESSAYIST AND AUTHOR

"The future belongs to those who believe in the beauty of their dreams."
ELEANOR ROOSEVELT (1884 - 1962) FIRST LADY OF THE USA 1933-1945

"All our dreams can come true – if we have the courage to pursue them."
WALT DISNEY (1901 - 1966) FILM PRODUCER AND ANIMATOR

INTRODUCTION

We spend a large proportion of our daily lives dreaming about what we are going to do and the reason we do this is to mentally rehearse and explore what we might encounter or how we might construct the future. The more we think about something the more we grow the mental pathways in our brains making us mentally and physically stronger.

Developing these mental pathways through daydreaming also provides other benefits. By thinking more positive thoughts we can make ourselves feel better and be more healthy; we can increase our luck through recognising opportunities which we have dreamt about previously; and respond more quickly to events when they happen.

In this chapter we will see how our brains have the ability to tune into the specific signals our senses convey to us. We will also investigate how our brains continue to grow and develop through mental and physical practice. And, importantly, consider how thinking about something is almost the same as physically doing it.

DAYDREAM BELIEVER

Did you ever find yourself daydreaming at school only to be brought harshly back to reality by the sharp tones of the teacher? It probably followed that you then felt guilty for not paying attention to what was happening in the classroom. It seems that we live in a culture where letting our minds wander is considered a bad thing and we are encouraged to keep our minds always focused.

Yet, daydreaming doesn't just happen when we are young. Have you ever found yourself staring into the distance and realised that for the past five minutes or so you have been lost in a dream world thinking about something which is really close to your heart? What took you

10

there? Why did you fall into this reverie when you should have been thinking about something else or doing something more urgent? The short answer is that your deep inner feelings surfaced and drew your attention to things which were important to you.

Too often, when we catch our mind wandering we hurriedly close the door on those positive thoughts and return to the immediate needs of everyday existence. But are we allowing ordinary mundane concerns distract us from a deeper and more meaningful life in which we can achieve so much more than we are presently doing? If the answer is, 'Yes', then we should listen more carefully to the dreams and then figure out a way of actually achieving them.

"Yet it is in our idleness, in our dreams, that the submerged truth sometimes comes to the top."
VIRGINIA WOOLF (1882-1941) AUTHOR

Dreams can be achieved and there is much evidence that some of the most influential discoveries and achievements known to humankind began with a dream. Perhaps the achievement originally began as the faintest notion of an idea which slowly grew and was eventually brought to fruition.

But there is a difference between those people who dream and are successful, and those who merely fantasise. Those who remain within a fantasy and never practically try to reach their ambitions are mostly deluding themselves and living in a never-never-land. But, and it is a big BUT, dreaming is a very important part of the process for reaching our desires and objectives. So we should not feel guilty about letting our minds wander to the things which are important to us. Sit back and enjoy the virtual journey around your dream world and then make it come true.

Daydreaming Is Good For Us

Another reason why we dream is that it feels good. It feels good to think about walking around our dream home; driving that dream car; sharing time with that dream partner; improving our health and appearance; or earning that large salary. When we think about something we desire our brain encourages the release of positive hormones which give us a positive feeling.

And now there is another powerful reason for giving ourselves permission to daydream. Using brain scanners, scientists in Canada, have surprisingly discovered that parts of the brain become more active when it is daydreaming. We may not necessarily use our brains in a focussed way when we daydream, but some parts of our brains associated with complex problem solving become very busy.

In fact, it would appear that we spend approximately one-third of our waking time daydreaming. Normally, we are not consciously aware that we are doing this because our attention is on the subject of our imaginations; however, it is possible to retrace our mental steps by thinking about what we have just been thinking. You can do this by just leaving a note to yourself perhaps by the computer screen, on the kitchen table or somewhere you frequently look at. Label the note: 'What am I thinking?' What you will find is that your mind is almost constantly pondering things deep within itself and operating as the guiding mechanism for your actions, behaviours and emotions .

Just as our physical muscles need to rest after strenuous exercise, so too do parts of our brains. Yet while, at one level, we are mentally and physically relaxing some other areas of our brain are very active and solving some of the challenges which we might face. The lesson is that we do not always have to concentrate on something to find a solution, if we leave it alone our brains will often daydream or work subconsciously to find the answer without us consciously trying.

THINKING IS OFTEN THE SAME AS DOING

For millennia people have thought that the processes of doing and thinking were entirely separate yet the invention of brain scanners which enable scientists to peer into the workings of the brain has revealed an astonishing finding. When we physically do something such as walking around our home certain areas of our brains connected with physical movement appear to light up as more blood flows to them. If we imagine walking around our home the same areas of our brains also light up. To our brains it appears that doing and thinking are remarkably similar.

Let's take an example. Just imagine that you are standing on the roof of a very tall skyscraper, and can look far to the horizon in all directions and see birds and aeroplanes in the sky above. Walk slowly towards the edge and as you get closer see more and more of the buildings that stretch down to the ground. As you get nearer the edge you begin to hear more clearly the noise of traffic in the street and the distant voices of people. You want to move away from the edge but force yourself to stand right on it with your toes desperately grasping to maintain a grip and prevent you falling. You are also aware of the wind which, although not strong, sometimes gusts and causes you to wobble and almost lose your balance. OK! Now step away from the edge and move right away from the canyon which you have been looking down.

How do you feel now – relieved? Just do a mental check, you might be perspiring, your heart almost certainly is beating a lot faster than before you began the exercise, and yet you are still sitting in your chair. This little exercise illustrates how powerful our imaginations are. We don't have to physically do something, we only have to think about something for it to have almost the same effect.

Growing Your Brain Power

If You Don't Use It You'll Lose It

When people break an arm or a leg it is normally set in plaster for a few weeks to help the bone heal. This immobilisation means that the limb cannot be used and the muscles tend to reduce in size and strength due to lack of exercise. Furthermore, this inactivity can result in the parts of the brain associated with arm or leg actions getting little use and also shrinking due to lack of action. Essentially, because the brain receives fewer stimuli it exercises less, and like our physical muscles it decreases. Fortunately, this issue is not permanent and people quickly recover the lost brain connections once they regain mobility.

It is not only when we break a limb that our brains can lose their sharpness, it also happens through general inactivity. If we do not regularly use our skills and knowledge then they are likely to decrease in capability or even disappear altogether. Most people are familiar with the experience of trying something they used to be good at only to discover that they were no longer as good as they thought which is because the area of our brain devoted to these activities has decreased in size.

It has also been found that the brains of rats which live in stimulating environments are much more developed and have more connections than those which live in more boring surroundings such as a cage. The strong message from these findings is that we can develop our minds if we regularly exercise our minds and bodies and also experience new and different situations. The same is especially true for children and older people who will benefit enormously from mental stimulation.

Grow Your Brain

There is a widespread belief that we have a certain number of brain cells or neurons and as we grow older these die and are not replaced. The consequence of this, we are told, is that our mental faculties decrease and our memories fade making us less effective. Also, it is argued that once we reach adulthood our brains are no longer plastic and flexible which allow us to learn easily; instead we are hardwired and have to make do with things as they are.

Fortunately, these beliefs are not entirely true. In fact, some parts of our brains continue to grow new cells which enable us to continue to learn new knowledge and develop new skills. And that is not all, what is just as important as possessing brain cells is the ability of the brain to make new connections between the cells so that we can link our experiences. Consider a recent experience, perhaps going shopping. Which route did you take to get there? Was the store crowded or quiet? Which goods did you buy? Did you see anyone you recognised etc? Those memories did not exist before you went to the store but they are there afterwards and they are all linked together so that you can have a detailed story about what you did.

In other words, you have made new connections between your brain cells and changed some of its wiring. This discovery that 'brain cells which fire together wire together' is called the Hebb Rule and the more we repeat or consciously revisit a memory the stronger the connections become.

The more a person practices an activity or learns something the better they become as the wiring in their brains becomes stronger and more elaborate. The stronger their brains become the better they will physically perform and the activity becomes more rewarding and enjoyable e.g. bowling strikes at the bowling alley; playing an instrument; speaking a foreign language; studying for an examination etc.

Mental and physical practice really do make people perform better. And, importantly, because they are mentally attuned to the possibility of something happening it also makes them luckier. Their mental preparation enables them to recognise opportunities and react very quickly to specific events which others would not even spot. Increasing luck is described in further detail in Chapter 5 and in the next section we will see how regular practice helps us be more successful in our lives.

Mental Practise Makes Perfect

Another myth is that we only use 10% of our brains and that if we could only use the other 90% as well we would be able to achieve remarkable things. This notion is very appealing to us because we all want to increase the capability of our brains, but it is not correct. The reality is that our brain is fantastic at helping us do and remember things and it has the capacity to achieve more if we train and develop it.

In fact, all parts of our brain serve a purpose and there do not appear to be areas of the brain which are dormant and are not used. The 'grey matter' which is found around the outer surface of the brain is used for some things and the 'white matter' below is used for other purposes. Some of this white matter surrounds the connecting wires which link different areas of the brain and the thicker this casing (myelin) the faster the signals will go around the brain.

This myelin casing becomes thicker the more we practise or think about an activity and it resembles the insulation around an electric cable. If we remove the insulation around an electric cable the electricity drains away into the ground. Likewise, if the myelin casing around the brain's connections deteriorates the brain's ability to function also decreases. Living healthily, eating nutritious food and taking exercise have the potential to improve the health of our brains and can even encourage brain cells to grow.

So why is this important? As we dream about various possibilities in the future we will gradually develop an understanding of what to do when an event actually happens. For example, if we have an upcoming important conversation with someone we will mentally rehearse, again and again, what we will say and how we will respond to the things they might argue. Instead of being tongue-tied we immediately know how to respond because we have mentally practiced this scenario many times. We can respond quickly because the connections have developed through rehearsal into major highways which are much easier and faster to conduct traffic than narrow winding side roads. If we had to think through things from the beginning we would be much slower and might not present our points of view in a very coherent way. Practice not only makes perfect it also speeds up the power of thought.

We call the making of new connections 'learning' and in the next few sections we will look at how the brain develops and even grows as we use it. In particular, we shall look at examples including taxi drivers, piano players, jugglers and sports people, and explore the powerful messages they have for each of us.

"We are what we repeatedly do. Excellence then, is not an action, but a habit."
ARISTOTLE (384 BC – 322 BC) GREEK PHILOSOPHER

TAXI DRIVERS

Satellite-navigation technology enables us to find our way to other towns and cities and once there guide us around streets which otherwise would become a nightmare maze. But this technology is not allowed if you want to take the London taxi-drivers' examination known as *The Knowledge*. To become a black cab driver on the streets of London it is necessary to learn 320 routes involving 25,000 streets and 20,000 landmarks. Learning these routes takes between two and four years and once a person passes *The Knowledge* they are entitled to drive anywhere in the Greater London area.

Possessing *The Knowledge* is very helpful because it allows the drivers to make rapid decisions about detours when they come across traffic jams or accidents. Satellite navigation, on the other hand, has limited

capability to respond to these sudden and sometimes extensive obstructions to a journey.

It would also appear that possessing *The Knowledge* has a significant effect on the size of a taxi-driver's brain. Research into the structure of their brains revealed that the part of the brain involved with spatial awareness and navigation of the environment is larger in the brains of taxi-drivers than the general public. Also, this part of the brain is larger in those taxi-drivers who had been driving for a longer period than those who have less experience.

It seems that if we practise a skill or increase our exposure to an area of information then the part of our brain associated with that will develop and grow. As this progresses our physical capabilities also grow and so we use them more. For example, the more we practise swimming the more the part of the brain associated with swimming grows thus helping us become even better at swimming. We create a virtuous circle and that is why taxi-drivers and people who regularly practise a skill get better and better.

A DREAM WITHIN A DREAM

Take this kiss upon the brow!
And, in parting from you now,
Thus much let me avow –
You are not wrong, who deem
That my days have been a dream;
Yet if hope has flown away
In a night, or in a day,
In a vision, or in none,
Is it therefore the less gone?
All that we see or seem
Is but a dream within a dream.

I stand amid the roar

Of a surf-tormented shore,

And I hold within my hand

Grains of the golden sand-

How few! yet how they creep

Through my fingers to the deep,

While I weep - while I weep!

O God! can I not grasp

Them with a tighter clasp?

O God! can I not save

One from the pitiless wave?

Is all that we see or seem

But a dream within a dream?

EDGAR ALLAN POE (1809 - 1849)

JUGGLING

Have you ever tried to do something physically complex such as learning to swim, ride a bicycle, serve at tennis, or juggle? It is not easy and often the harder we try the more difficult it becomes. Part of reason for this difficulty is due to trying to consciously coordinate all the different activities into one smooth movement. For example, when serving at tennis, we have to carefully throw the ball into the air with the right amount of height, and hit it with the racquet at the right time applying the correct amount of energy so that it flies over the net into the service box.

Trying to concentrate simultaneously on all the elements of a tennis serve overloads our conscious brains with too much information and they seize up. A much more effective way to learn to serve, swim, ride, or juggle is just to relax and let the inner subconscious brain get on with the job. The subconscious part of the brain has much more capacity and so finds this easier than if we try and concentrate on all the actions.

Once we stop trying to consciously control what we are doing the process becomes more natural and very soon we can learn the rudiments of juggling. At the beginning it seems unlikely that the skill of juggling will never happen and then gradually everything seems to click into place and it is possible to smoothly juggle without deep concentration.

At Oxford University, researcher Jan Scholz and colleagues scanned the brains of people who had learned to juggle and discovered that the part of the brain which handles visual and physical behaviours had become more highly organized. It is clear that as we learn our brains change shape and respond to the things we experience.

CRANIUM GYMNASIUM

MENTAL IMAGERY AND SPORT

Some years ago the author watched the Czech javelin thrower Jan Zelezny launch a javelin so powerfully that it went beyond the expected landing zone, almost skewering a TV commentator who thought he was at a safe distance, and achieving a new world record of 95.66m. It was such a phenomenal throw that it remains the second longest throw in history.

One of Zelezny's closest competitors at the time was the British sportsman, Steve Backley, who regularly challenged for the top position on the podium. To win at the highest level of sport requires complete dedication and giving 100% effort. Unfortunately, pushing the body to its limit can sometimes result in injuries which can destroy an athlete's career or prevent them from achieving their potential.

On one occasion shortly before a big international competition Backley injured his ankle and could not train. Normally this would put an athlete at a big disadvantage but Backley kept his mind in peak condition by mentally practising every tiny detail of his throw. He then repeated this a thousand times in all the major stadiums in the world with the result that when he physically returned to training he could resume from where he was before the injury happened rather than having to regain the lost skills. This use of mental imagery enabled Backley to win three Olympic medals in consecutive games and although now retired he still uses this dreaming skill in everyday life.

The use of imagination can create intense physical responses. Backley described how one athlete mentally pushed himself exceptionally hard during an imagined 400 metre run. When the athlete was not satisfied with his imagined performance he immediately ran another tough mental race which was something that would not happen in real life. The athlete exerted so much mental effort and experienced the event so vividly that he was physically sick!

GET PHYSICALLY STRONGER BY SITTING IN AN ARMCHAIR

We have seen how driving taxis, juggling and mentally running races can develop the connections between brain cells and even increase the size of parts of the brain. And there is even more - believe it or not but you can actually increase your physical strength by sitting in an armchair or even lying on the couch. Not possible, you might say, but you would be wrong.

In one experiment scientists gathered together three groups of people and measured the strengths of the little finger muscles in their left hands. The first group were given a physical exercise involving the finger muscles in the left hand. They repeated this muscle strengthening exercise during five sessions per week over a period of four weeks. The second group imagined doing the exercises for the same number of sessions; and the third group did absolutely nothing.

At the end of the month the strengths of the participant groups were measured again. As might be expected the little-finger strength of the third group which did nothing stayed the same. The finger strength of the first group which did the physical exercises increased by 30%, clearly showing that training is useful if we want to increase our strength and develop a skill.

But what was astonishing were the findings for the second group. Just thinking about doing the exercises increased their little-finger strength by an average of 22%! By only sitting and mentally exercising their brains these people were able to increase their physical strength which shows that if we want to train we should use our minds and our bodies. The old adage a healthy mind in a healthy body has some strong foundations.

We can use this discovery to improve our abilities in all sorts of areas. For example, when we are waiting for someone or something we can use this dead time to better purpose and mentally rehearse things which are important to us.

And, perhaps, the next time the boss catches you daydreaming you have a perfect excuse for what you are doing. You can say that you are mentally rehearsing and significantly improving that next presentation, report, physical activity etc!

DREAMS ARE REAL

Another example of regular practice affecting the structure of the brain was found by researchers at Harvard Medical School who recruited a group of volunteers and asked them to learn and practice a five-finger piano exercise. The volunteers attempted to do this in time with a 60-beats per minute metronome for two hours a day over a five day period.

At the end of each day the researchers examined the area of the volunteers' brains which controls the physical movement of their fingers. What they discovered was that the part of the brain devoted to these finger movements had begun to take over the surrounding areas of the brain, rather like daisies extending their roots across a garden lawn. It was found that the more a muscle was used the more the brain responded by allocating more space to that particular action.

Then, the researchers did something radical, they took another group of volunteers and asked them to simply imagine practising the piano exercise. Without moving their fingers they imagined playing the piano keys in their heads. The scientists then analysed the parts of the brain which controlled finger movement.

Astonishingly, it was discovered that the motor cortex which controls finger movement had actually expanded. Even though there had been no physical movement the mere use of thinking and imagination had developed the structure and operations of the brain. Mental training had caused similar effects to physical training.

EXPECTATIONS AFFECT OUTCOMES

THE SELF-FULFILLING PROPHECY

The extent to which a child succeeds in school is dependent on a number of factors including their own intellectual skills and motivation, their background, parental interest and the skills of the teachers. But there are also many other more hidden influences which affect the potential achievement of the child.

A number of experiments have been undertaken in schools to assess the impact of teacher expectations on the performance of the pupils. In one case, teachers were told that an assessment by researchers had revealed that certain children were 'intellectual bloomers' and would perform really strongly during the year. Later, all the children were assessed again and it was found that the bloomers had indeed performed more successfully on average than the other pupils.

The original prediction of academic success had proved correct, but the researchers hadn't properly explained to the teachers the real purpose of the research. In fact, the intellectual bloomers had been selected at random and were not high flyers. It seems that the expectations of the teachers influenced the performance of their pupils and where more was expected by the teachers more was given by the pupil. These findings have huge implications for all of us and can operate in a positive or negative way by raising or lowering achievement. If we expect certain levels of performance from our children, our partners or our work colleagues etc. they may live up to what we anticipate from them.

And it is not just others who are influenced by upbeat or harmful expectations. Consider the negative and positive statements below:

- I am never going to achieve anything in my life.
- I really don't want to work in this store for the rest of my life but I can't see any other opportunities.
- I'll never find a partner who is interested in the same things as me.
- I can never make a relationship last.
- There's no point in trying there are too many people in competition with me.

- If I keep going I'm sure I can achieve it.
- One day I will have my own place which perfectly suits my needs.
- I'm going to be a teacher, lawyer, nurse etc. which will enable me to help people and give me real job satisfaction.
- In the future I am going to be one of the best at...
- I know I can do it, I just have to remain focused.

Not only do our expectations influence the behaviours of others they can also influence our own performances. Within our heads our brains whirr away like computer programmes and these help us understand ourselves and the outside world. These mental programmes also guide our behaviour telling us what we like and don't like and what we think we can and can't do.

If we think that we can succeed at something we are likely to spot things that will help us reach our objective and we may also see or hear about other opportunities. On the other hand, if we are pessimistic and think that we are going to fail at something we may not even attempt it. The old saying, 'If you want to win the lottery, you have to buy a ticket' is true. Of course the chances of winning may be small but they are zero if you don't hold a ticket. In the same way, if you don't send an application for a job, volunteer for a position at work, ask that special person for a date, or be present at a meeting then the answer is probably "No!" As Woody Allen the actor and film director said, 'Half the secret of success in life is just showing up,' and this means that you are included in the lottery when opportunities are being discussed and shared out.

And this should send us the strong message that if we have high or low expectations about ourselves we may well achieve them. Which would you prefer to achieve – success or failure? The choice and result often would appear to be dependent on your mind set and attitude.

"For, he that expects nothing shall not be disappointed, but he that expects much – if he lives and uses that in hand day by day – shall be full to running over."
EDGAR CAYCE (1817 – 1945) PSYCHIC

IF YOU THINK IT WILL DO YOU GOOD...

The brain's role in our physical health should not be underestimated and there are examples where its effect is equal to and sometimes more powerful than conventional medicine. One of the most well-known examples of these is the placebo effect.

A placebo is an inactive pill or treatment (sometimes a sugar pill) which the patient believes is a real intervention. And, because they think that the pill or treatment will have a positive effect on them, the patient's physical condition actually improves. Therefore, when new drugs are being developed and tested, researchers often secretly give some patients a placebo instead of the real drug treatment in order to compare the effects of each. Sometimes the placebo has as much of an impact as the trial drug and without any side-effects.

However, a physician giving a placebo to a patient potentially deceives them into thinking that they are receiving genuine medication which can undermine the patient's trust in the doctor. Fortunately, there may be a possible solution which maintains the patient's trust. In one experiment, 40 patients were told they were being given a placebo and this was even printed on the bottle. Yet, three weeks later they still reported fewer symptoms than patients who had been given no pills whatsoever. It seems that even when they knew that a pill had no active ingredients it could still make them feel better.

So, our minds really do have an impact on our physical health. If we believe that something is going to make us feel good it may well do so.

SCULPTING YOUR BRAIN

Listen carefully! What can you hear? Vehicles passing? People laughing? Birds singing? Music playing? When you focus on a particular sound you can hear it more clearly and the reason you can do so is because you are sending a wave of electrical activity through your brain cells which are involved with hearing.

One minute they were just background noises, the next we can hear them very distinctly. This simple exercise illustrates just how clever our brains are in deciding which external signals to pay attention to and which to ignore. It also shows how the brain manages all the sensory signals which are bombarding us every day. No one truly knows how many signals our brains receive each day but if we actually paid attention to each of them there would be no time to do anything else.

Our brains also have the ability to switch off those sensory signals which we are very familiar with e.g. making our routine journey to work becomes so automatic that when we arrive we can remember almost nothing of the journey. This process of habituation enables us to disregard unimportant minor details and give our attention to other things which we consider important such as planning a meeting with a colleague.

So, our brains have learned to pay attention to things which we consider important to us. It might be our loved ones, music, football, food, things which are new or different etc. and because we give more attention to these things the areas of our brains associated with them grow in size. And the more these parts of our brain grow the greater the ability we have to see, hear and analyse these things. For example, if we develop an interest in classical music we create a virtuous circle in which we will increasingly be able to hear and appreciate more aspects of what we are hearing etc.

THE COCKTAIL PARTY EFFECT

Our brains not only have the ability to focus on specific things such as giving our exclusive attention to some music or watching the TV, they also monitor many other things without us even being aware that they are doing so. Have you ever attended a noisy event with many people talking loudly and perhaps music blaring in the background? Whenever we find ourselves in these situations it is often necessary to pay close attention to what people are saying or we will lose track of the conversation. The result of this concentration is that we filter and exclude from our consciousness all the other intrusive noises so as not to confuse our brain with too much clutter.

This ability to concentrate on something and exclude other distractions is a highly important one, but there is also a parallel operation happening at the same time. Perhaps you have noticed when you are concentrating on a speaker and excluding other sounds in the noisy environment, that you hear someone else outside your group say your name? This didn't just happen by chance e.g. the music temporarily dropped in volume. What actually happened was that your brain was listening to ALL the sounds within earshot and filtering out all those noises which it considered irrelevant.

However, when someone uses our name it generally indicates that they are trying to attract our attention, or may be saying things about us which we may or may not like. Therefore, our brain allows our name through the filter and enables us to tune into things which might be important to us. Rather like a coffee machine prevents the coffee grounds from spoiling the smooth taste of a cappuccino, the subconscious brain sieves the information it receives and allows through things which are important to us.

WHY WE FORGET

Finally, in this chapter, it is helpful to consider why our brains tend to forget things. Our memories enable us to store information and recall it when we need it; however, this process is not perfect and we often forget information. This forgetfulness is not necessarily a bad thing, although if we are repeatedly forgetting details which have happened recently then it may be a good idea to visit a health professional.

Our memories are influenced by stress, things we don't wish to remember, and other causes. But, possibly the most major reason we forget things is that our brain, although the most powerful computer on earth, has a limited capacity and cannot contain everything with which we come into contact. Just think how much detail there is in the world – take a look at a tree, a large building or around a room. Now close your eyes and try and remember every single thing that you saw. Impossible isn't it?

We have thousands of thoughts each day but we only pay attention to a small number of them. The rest we cast away without noticing. So forgetting things isn't always a sign that our brains aren't functioning correctly. Our brains are designed to pay attention to the things which we consider important and ignore things which we consider have no relevance. This enables us to focus on what friends are saying to us even when there is loud distracting music in the background. If we absorbed everything we encountered our brains would become overloaded and we would not be able to function. For example, if we are crossing a road and concentrating on all the little details around us we might supress other more important things such as the bus heading directly at us!

DREAM SUMMARIES

- All things, we create, begin with a dream inside a person's head.

- Daydreaming and letting our minds wander are natural behaviours.

- Daydreaming makes us feel good through the release of natural hormones.

- Thinking about something and doing something activate the same areas of the brain.

- Parts of our brains continue to grow brain cells even when we are older.

- When we learn something new our brain cells make new connections and can even grow if we regularly practice a skill such as navigating around London, swimming, juggling etc.

- Mental rehearsal can make us physically stronger.

- Our brains have the ability to let us concentrate on specific signals such as a person's voice, a bird in the sky etc.

- Our subconscious brains are constantly scanning for information that is important to us even though we are not consciously aware of it.

- It is not the signals which we receive but the way our brain interprets them.

- Our memories do not remember everything which allows us to store the more important information.

2
DREAMS AND FEELINGS

"Never let the future disturb you. You will meet it, if you have to, with the same weapons of reason which today arm you against the present."
MARCUS AURELIUS ANTONINUS AUGUSTUS (121 – 180 AD) ROMAN EMPEROR

INTRODUCTION

People spend about one third of their time daydreaming and thinking about possible events in the future. Negative thoughts about the future cause anxiety and worry and the stress produces hormones such as cortisol which can be damaging if it occurs over long periods. However, this is not to say that anxiety is necessarily a bad thing. Nature has taught us to keep our eyes open for trouble, and anxiety makes us prepare in advance so that we can then avoid some of the bad things which might otherwise befall us.

Conversely, when people optimistically look forward to something in the future their brains encourage the release of chemicals which give them a positive feeling of wellbeing. This positive feeling then encourages us carry out the action and achieve a result.

It would appear that there are three ways of dreaming about the future: in a negative way, a positive way, and a neutral way. Negative thoughts encourage anxiety and worry; positive thoughts encourage hope; and neutral thoughts help us analyse things in a rational manner. This chapter will begin with an exploration of negative perceptions about the future and then look at how you can view things from a positive perspective. Then, in the following chapter we will consider ways for you to take control of your dreams and you future.

ANXIETY AND WORRY

WORRY AND FEAR

Anxiety is a state of mind where a person feels unable to fully control or avoid negative future events. Although this emotion is sometimes considered negatively it can be a constructive one which drives a person to take preventive action or be on the lookout for possible danger. In this way it can make a person's life safer and more comfortable. The only problem is when a person obsessively worries all the time making them become pessimistic and creating high levels of stress. Anxiety and worry are also bad habits if they are not linked to physical action which attempts to resolve the problem. Worry without action does not resolve a problem and the result is that it continues to nag away in the brain.

Sometimes we let our minds run away when we are anxious about something. The internal conversation goes something like this: "The bus is late and so I will get to work late. Then there won't be enough time to prepare for that meeting and then the boss will shout at me. And the firm is doing badly and I will be the first to be fired, and then... and then..."

When we find ourselves in this downward spiral of negative thoughts we need to take time out from them and give ourselves some breathing space. The danger is that we become so locked into a train of thoughts there is no further space inside our heads for any counterfactual thinking. Our brains are so filled with negative thoughts and emotions it becomes very difficult to leap out of these tramlines which restrict our thinking and replace them with something more constructive.

Most people experience negative thinking and even feel very down at some time in their lives and it is believed that this may serve a purpose. Life events such as bereavements, illness, and separation affect our emotional equilibrium and leave us vulnerable to making wrong decisions or acting impulsively which might put us in danger. Feeling down is nature's way of protecting us by making us withdraw a little from life's hustle and bustle and thus giving us time and space to recover our usual balance.

Essentially worry is the mental rehearsal of the possible things which might go wrong during a future situation. By thinking through our options and possible solutions to life's challenges we increase the potential for behaving in a manner which will best suit the circumstances. In this way we can anticipate possible dangers and make a diversion or find a way of handling the problem. As the writer Samuel Johnson said:

"Fear is implanted in us as a preservative from evil; but its duty, like that of any other passions, is not to overbear reason, but to assist it."

Everyone is different and each of us has varying degrees of resilience depending on what we are facing and the load we have to carry. What may frighten one person may not cause any concern to another and vice versa. The word for this is idiosyncratic – it depends on the person.

Therefore, in order to regain control of our thoughts we have to lift ourselves away from our negative thinking to a more rational approach. Undoubtedly, people are sometimes faced with some extremely difficult challenges regarding their health and their futures. Yet pure negative thinking is very unlikely to resolve anything unless it is attached to action. The thought processes of those locked into negative thinking are rather like the old fashioned records which got stuck and kept replaying the same bit of music again and again. If we find that our thinking is too negatively focused it can often help to share these thoughts with a good friend, counsellor, and/or health professional and also ask ourselves some questions:

- Am I trapped in my own way of thinking?
- Is this thinking preventing me from finding a solution?
- What are the true facts about this situation?
- How likely is this to happen?
- What would other people say about my fears?
- How would other people manage this situation?
- Can I apply some of their solutions to my own situation?
- What is the worst that could happen and how might it be managed?
- What did I do and how did I cope the last time I had thoughts like these?
- How will I feel about this in a year's time?

38

The danger is that our fears may so inhibit us that we do not live our dreams. People who live in dread of a future event can become overwhelmed with what might happen that this paralyzes them so much that they do not make any attempt to reduce or even avoid the future situation. The result of this inaction can be that an avoidable situation becomes certain to happen. This fear of fear was described by US President F.D. Roosevelt in his inaugural speech during the Great Depression of the 1930s:

> *"So, first of all, let me assert my firm belief that the only thing we have to fear is fear itself – nameless, unreasoning, unjustified terror which paralyzes needed efforts to convert retreat into advance."*

PESSIMISM

Pessimism is the perspective which holds that things will turn out for the worse in the future and pessimistic people generally hold little confidence or hope about the outcome of things. This doesn't mean that these people are necessarily feeling down, it might just be that they choose to expect less from the world. This is a form of defensive pessimism in which the person adopts a pessimistic perspective so that they are not disappointed. The reasoning behind this approach to life is that if you expect the worst you will sometimes be pleasantly surprised when things turn out not to be so bad. The argument goes that if you are too optimistic then you are likely to be disappointed more often.

The familiar analogy of 'the glass is half-full or half-empty' illustrates how people can assess and interpret life. 'She's a glass half-full person' is taken to mean someone who can see the positive side of things while the opposite is true for those who concentrate more on the empty half of the glass. What this symbolises is that the contents of the glass don't change but people's interpretations do.

This 'half-full, half-empty' perspective illustrates that we possess a choice about how we wish to interpret the world. Often people believe that the way they see the world is the one true perspective and that other people's views are not as accurate as their own. In fact, there are many ways of seeing the world and the important thing to recognise is that we all possess a choice about which perspective to take.

Importantly, adopting a negative outlook reduces the possibility that we will be on the outlook for positive things and therefore we are less likely to see opportunities. In Chapter 5 chance and luck are discussed in greater detail.

"A pessimist sees the difficulty in every opportunity; an optimist sees the opportunity in every difficulty."
WINSTON CHURCHILL (1874 – 1965) POLITICIAN

WHY WORRY?

Being a pessimist can be put to good use if it involves preparing for negative eventualities. Conversely, a naively positive person may be so convinced that things will turn out for the best that they make no plans or allow for any contingency measures. Indeed, optimism is probably not the best strategy if the cost of failure is likely to be high. In some ways this latter perspective illustrates a limited ability to dream where only a positive fantasy world seems possible.

The danger of holding a pessimistic outlook about the future is that this makes us focus on negative outcomes and this can lead to fear and worry. And the more we worry the more we focus on a negative future and disregard the possibility that things may turn out positively.

People often irrationally think that if they worry about something enough then this will help – it probably won't! There are good reasons why we worry and that is to make us prepare for something which might happen in the future. If we prepare ourselves in advance then there is a greater potential for things to turn out for the better. If we have examinations coming up then our anxiety about them may make us study harder and thus get a better grade. If we are too mentally relaxed and laid back there is less of a driving force to make us work hard which might cause poorer results.

There is one thing definite about the future – it is uncertain! And this uncertainty can cause people anxiety where they worry about possible or probable events which make them feel bad. Also, the more they feel bad the more they have negative thoughts about the event which sometimes drives them into a negative spiral.

Essentially, there are two types of worry. We can worry about problems which are suitable for problem solving and we can worry about those over which we have no control. An example of the first might be concern about an upcoming job interview – we can rehearse our answers before the event. The other type of anxiety might be related to the possibility of an earthquake about which little can be done. As the prayer says:

> *"Grant me the serenity to accept the things I cannot change, the courage to change the things I can, and the wisdom to know the difference."*

The important thing is not to waste energy in worrying, but rather use it to good effect by thinking about a solution and / or doing something which will prevent the event happening or at least reduce it. It would seem that a balance between pessimism and optimism might be the best perspective where we prepare for the worst and expect the best.

LEARNED HELPLESSNESS

Much of our behaviour is based on our personal experiences. For example, if we meet many honest and caring people we are more likely to trust people in general. Alternatively, if we come across many people who lie, steal or cheat we are more likely to believe that people cannot be trusted. These experiences do not mean that all people are good or that all people are bad, what we should learn from these experiences is to develop a little caution. There are mostly kind, honest people in the world but some are best avoided.

There is a danger, though, that if we have a great many negative experiences this will colour our perception of humanity. Moreover, if we suffer too many negative life experiences we may begin to lose our sense of control and just accept things the way they are no matter how bad they seem. This has been called 'learned helplessness' and basically involves us giving up hope of being able to control circumstances with the result that we become passive, introspective and depressed. What has been found from research is that some people do not succumb to these disheartening experiences but bounce back and find a way around the obstacles – these people were found to be more optimistic.

So what can we learn from all of this? What we think will enormously influence our behaviour and if we think that things are going to remain bad they probably will. Alternatively, if we can develop a more positive outlook, a 'learned optimism' then we are more likely to try out different strategies.

The psychologist, Martin Seligman, suggested that we should sometimes challenge our thinking, for example, the ABCDE approach:

> Adversity: Another driver cuts in front of you.
> Belief: Your self-talk says: "That driver was aggressive and inconsiderate."
> Consequence: We become angry and blow the horn.
> Disputation: Challenge your initial thoughts – perhaps they didn't see you or were distracted by something else.
> Energization: We are energised by thinking about the event and continue our journey safely and are not distracted by what happened.

MIND AND BODY IN HARMONY

When we have a cold or some other illness they, not surprisingly, can make us feel bad. And, as we have discovered, thinking about something negative can also make us feel physically worse because this causes the body to release hormones which influence our feelings of wellbeing.

And, there is yet another factor which can affect our feelings. If you have ever marvelled at the almost true to life behaviour and expressions of the characters in films such as *Toy Story*, and *Monsters Inc.* you can thank the researchers Paul Ekman and Wallace Friesen who developed the Facial Action Coding System. Over a period of eight years and with great attention to detail they identified all the muscles which are used in generating facial expressions. Much of this research involved making the expressions themselves and then recording which muscles were used.

Once, while undertaking their research both researchers started to feel bad and one said that he couldn't continue because he felt so terrible. This experience was not normal because neither of them had any obvious reason to feel this way so they both started exploring why this might have happened. Eventually they realised that because they had spent all that day making negative expressions they had triggered the body's autonomic responses thus making them feel unhappy.

So, as we have found, not only does thinking something negative have an effect on ourselves, just pulling negative faces can make us feel worse. It is easier to smile because it uses fewer muscles than frowning so if we wish to feel better the answer is to smile. And our smiles will be received by other people who are more likely to respond positively and create a virtuous circle as can be seen in the next section.

> *"We are all in the gutter, but some of us are looking at the stars."*
> OSCAR WILDE (1854 – 1900) IRISH WRITER AND POET

THE BEHAVIOURAL CYCLE

When a person is feeling good about themself this attitude tends to be translated into positive behaviour e.g. smiling, being confident etc. This behaviour, in turn, influences people around them who respond in a more positive manner making the original person feel even more positive. This process results in a virtuous cycle of positive esteem and feelings which can be seen in the positive behavioural cycle diagram.

Conversely, when a person is not feeling good about themselves this tends to influence their self-esteem which is then reflected in their behaviour e.g. being downcast, looking sad. Other people only see this negative behaviour and often respond by taking into account the behaviour which they see, for example, they might moderate their behaviour to be more sensitive and low key. This may result in a cycle

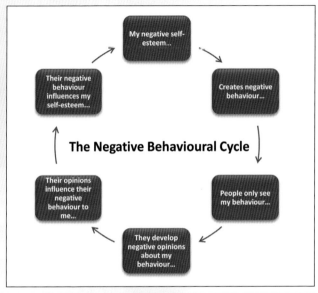

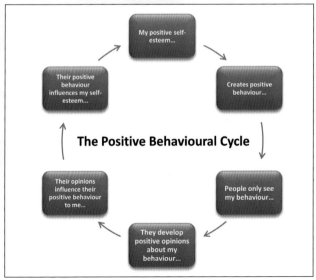

of low esteem which becomes reinforced creating a downward spiral and can be seen in the negative behavioural cycle diagram.

Confidence tends to inspire confidence and vice versa, so for managers, parents, partners etc. it is often beneficial to appear positive when inside we are feeling anything but. By appearing positive we will receive more positive feedback which helps to make us feel better. Also, putting a brave face on things can sometimes improve the outcome of situations where people around us respond more constructively than if they perceive us to be unsure or doubtful.

"To enjoy good health, to bring true happiness to one's family, to bring peace to all, one must first discipline and control one's own mind. If a man can control his mind he can find the way to Enlightenment, and all wisdom and virtue will naturally come to him."
BUDDHA

Of course, there may still be days when we need a hug or feel like having quiet personal time. But the more we are aware of our emotions the easier it is to understand how and why we are feeling a particular way and so handle them to some extent. This is often called emotional intelligence and the more we are emotionally aware of our own emotions and those of other people the more we can manage our lives. Indeed, emotional intelligence and resilience have a larger effect on our lives and success than intelligence.

Emotions tend to be contagious and so positive behaviour encourages positive behaviour and negative behaviour encourages negative behaviour. Being positive with other people will normally be reciprocated and will receive positive behaviour in return. We can kick-start a positive cycle of behaviour by smiling and appearing confident and so manage our emotions and influence those in people around us.

DREAMS

I have been happy, tho' in a dream.

I have been happy - and I love the theme:

Dreams! in their vivid coloring of life,

As in that fleeting, shadowy, misty strife

Of semblance with reality, which brings

To the delirious eye, more lovely things

Of Paradise and Love - and all our own!

Than young Hope in his sunniest hour hath known.

EDGAR ALLAN POE (1809 - 1849)

MIRROR, MIRROR ON THE WALL

There are different ways in which we can use our imagination. For example, we can go back in time and imagine a different ending to an event. We can also go forward in time and dream about things in the future; and, we can also observe people in real time and imagine what they are thinking.

Have you ever flinched in sympathy as you saw someone accidently injure themselves? Or perhaps you found yourself becoming emotionally affected as you watched the actors in a movie? We have the ability to imagine and understand what other people are experiencing even though we are not directly involved. We call this affinity to the feelings of other people empathy, and it is a valuable skill in helping us understand and get along with others.

Some years ago Italian scientists were investigating how the brain worked when they noticed something remarkable. As one of them reached for some food, the brain of a watching monkey was activated in the area also involved with reaching. Somehow, the activities of the scientists were being monitored by the monkey and it was as if a light bulb had been switched on in the scientists' brains. They realised that humans might also have the same ability to mentally respond to the actions of other people and they discovered what are called mirror neurons – cells in the brain which respond to what we see happening in others.

It appears that when we watch someone do something the same areas of our brains are activated as if we are actually doing it and so we can imagine how they feel. If they smile our mirror neurons for smiling are also activated and make us feel the same way. If they frown or wrinkle their noses at the taste of some food etc we share their experience. This ability to empathise with other people helps us to socialise and establish connections with other people. It also enables us to learn from others so that, for example, if they make a mistake, we can learn from their mistake and not do the same thing.

This ability to figure out and also experience what another person is feeling is a form of emotional contagion which can even influence larger groups of people. When a group of friends are sitting together they can all tune into the experiences described by one of them. On a larger scale at music concerts and sports events etc. people can become carried away by the shared atmosphere.

HOPE FOR THE FUTURE

ALWAYS LOOK ON THE BRIGHT SIDE OF LIFE

Optimism is about having hope and confidence that things will turn out well in the future. Above we discussed how 'the glass half-full or half-empty' was a choice about how we see the world. Of course, some people are more naturally disposed to seeing the world more negatively or positively, but this need not necessarily be a fixed condition.

Have you noticed that when you are thinking about something good in your life you start to feel more positive? The reason is that the brain encourages the release of positive hormones which make us feel better; therefore, if we want to feel better we should think positive things. Similarly, if we have negative thoughts the body produces hormones which can help it to respond to threats; but if we are continually stressed these hormones can cause physical damage to us.

The psychologist Martin Seligman described how in 1932 the mother superior of the Sisters of Notre Dame in the United States asked all novice nuns to write an autobiographical description of themselves. The descriptions were archived and more recently they were analysed by psychologists who assessed how positive they were. Surprisingly, the degree of positive feelings which the nuns possessed early in their life was a reasonably accurate predictor of how long they would live; those nuns who were more positive lived longer than those who were less positive. It would appear that we live longer and have better health because we are happy; and not just that we are happy because we have better health and live longer.

Yet it sometimes happens that despite thinking positive thoughts negative things happen in our lives. The upside of this means that at least the journey was more enjoyable than if we had been having negative thoughts all the time. Looking on the bright side of life would appear to improve our health and also give us increased opportunities. If we have an optimistic outlook on life we will tend to have an expectation that something positive might happen to us and therefore be on the lookout for opportunities. On the other hand, if we tend to be pessimistic then we are more likely to switch off to the opportunities we encounter and thus miss them. It is valuable to recognise that, in many respects, life is not so much about what happens to us but how we respond to events.

> *"The essence of optimism is that it takes no account of the present, but it is a source of inspiration, of vitality and hope where others have resigned; it enables a man to hold his head high, to claim the future for himself and not to abandon it to his enemy."*
> DIETRICH BONHOEFFER (1906 – 1945) GERMAN PASTOR

Positive Thoughts

Keep your thoughts positive, because your thoughts
become your words.
Keep your words positive, because your words
become your behaviour.
Keep your behaviour positive, because your behaviour
become your habits.
Keep your habits positive, because your habits
become your values.
Keep your values positive, because your values
become your destiny.

Mahatma Gandhi (1869 – 1948) Father of the Nation, India

CAMP ESPERANZA

One day in 2010 a group of 33 men set off for work as usual but this day turned out to be one which changed their lives forever. They descended 2,300 feet (700 metres) underground at the St Jose mine near Copiapó, Chile in the arid Atacama Desert and began their shift mining for copper. However, the roof suddenly collapsed and they were trapped deep underground.

At first the dust from the collapse made it very difficult to see anything and it greatly irritated their eyes, but as it settled they slowly made their way through the lower levels of the mine which were unaffected by the rockfall, and gathered at an emergency shelter. Miraculously they discovered that all were uninjured and they began to consider what might become of them. There were ventilation shafts through which the miners might have escaped but the ladders were missing and also there were further rock movements which meant they could not be used.

During the early days of their imprisonment they feared that they might never be rescued and that they would all slowly die from starvation. Each man was left alone with his thoughts about the potential consequences of what might happen. It was a very harrowing and desperate time and the miners, assailed by doubts and dark thoughts, took turns supporting one another. As one miner later described: "I was with God, and with the Devil -- and God took me."

There was little they could do to rescue themselves but they needed to manage the situation and increase their chances of survival. The miners decided to organize themselves to maintain the mine, look after each other and support morale. They introduced a system of one man, one vote to make decisions about how to increase their chances of survival. Water seeped into the mine shaft which the miners drank and the shelter held food supplies for three days but by careful rationing they managed to make them last for two weeks. Despite this the miners each lost an average of 18lbs (8kg).

The lack of communication meant that the miners did not know what rescue attempts might be tried or whether they would ever be reached. On the surface families, friends and rescue workers rushed to the mine as soon as the details of the disaster become known but no one knew if the miners had survived the rock collapse and the people were desperate for any news. A camp was quickly established where families waited for news about the rescue attempts but as the days passed the possibility of the miners surviving declined. However, until there was definite information that they had succumbed the families prayed and tried to raise their spirits by calling the growing village Campamento Esperanza – Camp Hope. Thirty two Chilean, and one Bolivian, flags were flown each representing the nationalities of the lost men and the hopes and dreams of the waiting families.

The rescue efforts involved drilling several bore holes to try and find the miners, however, this was very difficult because of the depth of the miners and the hardness of the rock which caused drills to drift away from the intended direction. Fourteen days into the rescue a borehole reached a space which the rescuers thought the miners, if they had survived, might be trapped. Disappointingly no signs of life were discovered.

On day 17 the rescuers raised the drill and discovered a message taped to it. It read, "Estamos bien en el refugio, los 33." "We are well in the shelter, the 33." This news gave everyone new hope and as the French proverb says,

"Hope is the dream of a man awake."

Food, water, belongings and equipment were swiftly transported down to the miners and efforts were then focused on drilling a wider shaft.

This widening operation caused rock fragments to fall down the shaft and in all, some 700 tons had to be removed by the miners as they waited for their rescue.

The boring of a wider rescue shaft took a considerable time because of technical challenges, the hardness of the rock and various obstacles on route such as a metal girder from old mine workings. During this period the family members maintained a vigil as they waited for the release of their loved ones. Initially, the rescuers did not tell the miners how long it would take to rescue them because they felt that it might dishearten them. But a few days later they were informed about the duration of their entrapment so that they could keep their morale and could adjust their minds to the long wait.

Eventually, after a record 69 days of being entombed, the miners were hauled up the rescue shaft inside a 21 inch (54 cm) wide capsule. One by one they travelled up to the surface and were greeted by a doctor, the President of Chile, their families and television cameras transmitting pictures to a billion people around the world. The shift foreman, like the captain of a ship, was the last to be rescued.

This adventure not only captured the attention of those directly involved with the events it also attracted attention from across the globe. The reason for this was the appeal of people keeping their hopes and dreams in the face of a potential disaster. Seeing hope also gave hope to those who saw it and transferred the lessons to their own lives. A daughter was born to one of the miners while he was trapped and she was called Esperanza – Hope!

DREAM SUMMARIES

- Anxiety and worry are emotions related to possible negative future situations.

- Worry can also make people feel down and not take action through a learned helplessness.

- Anxiety can be useful because it can make us take action to alleviate or avoid possible future challenges.

- We have brain cells called mirror neurons which help us understand and feel what other people are thinking and feeling.

- People who are more positive tend to spot opportunities more often and are luckier.

- Optimistic people may be healthier and live longer – we can learn to be optimistic.

- Hope is a powerful motivator.

3
TAKING CONTROL OF
YOUR FUTURE

"If one advances confidently in the direction of one's dreams, and endeavours to live the life which one has imagined, one will meet with a success unexpected in common hours."
HENRY DAVID THOREAU (1817 – 1862) AUTHOR, PHILOSOPHER

INTRODUCTION

In previous chapters we have explored how our dreams and thoughts can shape the physical structure of our brains making them grow and increasing our abilities. In this chapter we will build on these findings and look at how our thoughts influence our feelings and how our feelings can influence our thoughts.

There is a belief among many people that their thoughts and feelings direct their behaviour, yet if we monitor our thoughts we can observe them rather like an air-traffic controller observes airplanes and guides them to their destinations. Likewise, our minds can not only observe our thoughts they can also direct our thoughts where we wish them to go. Understanding this ability to control our thoughts can lead to a more healthy and stress-reduced life and can help us achieve our dreams.

In this chapter we will also explore examples of people who have used daydreaming to escape the physical confines in which they find themselves.

WHO IS IN CONTROL?

Find a quiet, peaceful place and just sit and observe the thoughts which freely enter your mind. There is no need to deeply analyse these thoughts, just act like an independent spectator making a note of them and seeing which ones are positive, negative or neutral. While you are doing this pay attention to those thoughts which tend to draw you in and begin to make you feel a particular way.

The fact that you could observe your thinking demonstrates that you are distinct from the thoughts that are flying around in your head. Your consciousness and awareness of your thoughts is rather like a busy flight controller who is directing and lining up airplanes to land at a busy airport. You can choose to give priority to some thoughts and ignore others which you consider irrelevant.

In other words, thinking is not something which independently happens to us as many people believe. Instead, thinking is something which we do, and we can control the thoughts inside our head should we choose to do so. This is the opposite of allowing our thoughts to control us, and this perspective puts us in the driving seat where we can choose the direction we wish to travel.

For example, briefly think about what you would really like to eat for your evening meal. Very quickly your mind tunes into what you would find most appetising and this might make your mouth water. What you have just done is to direct you brain to dream about a really tasty meal; you have chosen what to think about.

Undoubtedly, internal thoughts have the power to significantly influence the way we feel, but these are just thoughts. Are you in control of your mind, or is your mind in control of you?

FEELINGS FOLLOW THOUGHTS...

Have you ever noticed how one moment you can be in a really good mood and then suddenly your emotions drop like a ton of bricks as you think of something negative? When we think about something negative our brains encourage the release of hormones which tend to make us have more negative thoughts, which make us feel worse and so on. This feedback loop makes us feel worse and has the potential to drive people into a downward spiral.

Fortunately, the reverse is also true. If we have positive thoughts they cause the brain to produce 'good' hormones which make us feel better. This begins to develop a virtuous circle where we change our thoughts which change our feelings and which change our lives. What these situations reveal is that it is our thoughts which frequently trigger our feelings. So if we can change our thoughts from negative ones to positive ones we can influence how we feel.

A simple exercise will illustrate what we are talking about. Try to feel angry without having angry thoughts. Try to feel rejected without having thoughts of rejection. Try to feel sad without having sad thoughts. It's impossible, isn't it?

The clear message coming from this exercise is that our thoughts influence our feelings which is why we often try to distract children's thinking away from one thing to another when they are upset. If we can do it for children then we ought to be able to do it for ourselves! For example, we do this when we say to ourselves, "There's no need to worry about it now, I'll deal with it later," or ,"What's the point of worrying?"

...AND THOUGHTS FOLLOW FEELINGS

Our brains are exceptionally complex and despite the amazing technology and pioneering research which is being conducted by cognitive scientists there is still an enormous amount which is still unknown. The mysteries deep within our brains are still a long way from being discovered let alone explained. However, we do have an increasing understanding of how we think and much of it is confirming what the ancient philosophers from Greece and Rome were able to discern through observing and thinking about people's behaviour.

So, where do our thoughts come from? Essentially, our thoughts tend to originate from two main sources: internally within ourselves and externally from the environment around us. Internal thoughts often begin with our need for food, drink, warmth, shelter, love, respect, and peace. If we do not have these things they create a craving which

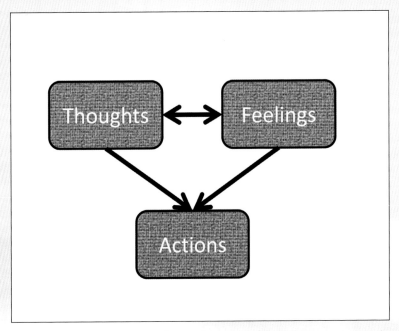

continues to occupy our minds until it is satisfied. For example, if we are thirsty it is very difficult to concentrate on other things until we have had a glass of water or perhaps a cup of coffee.

What often happens once we have satisfied one craving is that another desire or longing then enters our minds, perhaps this might be for the company of friends or a loved one. It can often seem that we are continually chasing our next desire rather than appreciating the moment.

The other main source of our thoughts is the environment around us which provides an almost limitless source of sensory signals to our senses. Just sit quietly where you are and begin to take in all the sights, sounds, physical sensations and aromas around you. Pay attention to each of these in turn. You might want to begin with a consideration of the things which you can see; look at each one in turn; what shape is it, what colour(s) does it have. Then consider the sounds which there are and, again taking each one in turn, single one out to pay special attention to. Next, consider the things which you can feel: they might be the feel of the chair underneath you, the clothes you are wearing, this book which you are holding etc.

As you do this exercise you might notice that one thought triggers another and then another. Often, different thoughts get mixed up together and stimulate further new ideas. Very soon you are far away from your original thought and it is often difficult to retrace your mental steps more than a few stages. This can happen when you digress from a subject and then realise you have lost the thread of your main thoughts.

During the exercise above you might have noticed when focussing on a particular object that there were increasing levels of detail which you could pay attention to. The more you concentrated the more you could observe. What also happened was that all the other things in the room or location faded away and you lost them from your attention.

This focus on detail is one of the strategies used by many successful people. They tend to keep their eyes on the ball or their objective and disregard all the other things which might distract them. It takes self-discipline and close attention to detail in order to achieve things. Otherwise, our energies are dissipated in all sorts of directions leaving us with little strength left to achieve our overall vision.

This is not to say that other things aren't important, there are many things which we need to give attention to in order to have a balanced lifestyle and achieve a feeling of wellbeing. Indeed, there are many things which are jostling for priority and we have to choose which are the most important and deal with them. One way to do this is to identify and list all the things we feel that we need to do and then prioritise them in terms of which are important and which are urgent. We can then deal with them in a more logical order.

So what can we learn from these discussions about thoughts and feelings? Thoughts have a powerful influence on our feelings and if we can monitor our thoughts and direct them we can also alter our feelings. Similarly, our feelings can influence our thoughts, for example, we might notice that we are feeling a little down and wonder why this might be, and then soon afterwards we get a cold or some other condition. There is a dance going on between our thoughts and our feelings but we often have the power to choose which music is playing in the background.

MIND CONTROL

MIND OVER MATTER

Imagine yourself gently running on a treadmill which is moving at a slow pace. Gradually the speed increases and when the incline is raised it makes it feel like you are running up a steep hill. As you do this mental exercise you may have noticed that your breathing has increased and if you had been monitoring your heart you would have found that it was also beating faster.

Research has found that even when we are resting in a chair our physical state is altered by what we are thinking about. If we have relaxed thoughts then we are likely to be more physically relaxed and if we have angry thoughts we are more highly energised and ready for action. These physical responses might have worked successfully in the far forgotten past when our ancestors had to run away from woolly mammoths but it is much less suitable in the present world where we can no longer beat someone over the head with a club, no matter how much we might wish to!

If we persistently continue with highly emotional and stressful thoughts they will increase our chances of physical illnesses such as stomach ulcers and mental illness. Changing our thoughts and self-talk can alter our physical responses and decrease the chance of a heart attack.

When we talk to ourselves these thoughts activate the same areas of the brain which would be busy if we were physically doing it. We are responsible for the thoughts, images and dreams inside our heads and these can create emotions and physical sensations. Monitoring our self-talk is a powerful means to creating a better world for ourselves.

CHOOSE YOUR FEELINGS

Have you noticed how some days it is much easier to deal with things than at other times? Sometimes we may have loads of energy and find things a breeze; the next we are tired and stressed and it all becomes too much to handle. The circumstances haven't changed markedly but our ability to manage the situation has. What this means is that our attitude to things not only varies but also influences how we interpret events. If we can change our attitude then we can change how we feel about a particular situation.

Imagine a great soccer match between two really skilful teams with the game closely balanced at 2-2 with only a few minutes to play and both attacking to get the winning goal. Just before the referee blows the final whistle one team scores a spectacular winner and their supporting fans go wild with excitement. At the other end of the stadium, there is only stunned silence. What happened in the game was the same for both sets of fans but it was their perspectives which altered their feelings about the outcome. For some, the result of the game would carry over into the rest of the week making it miserable. For others, the result would be disappointing but they would bounce back and get on with their lives, and perhaps say, "Next time we will beat them."

Another story illustrates how we have a choice about how we interpret events in our lives. One morning two work colleagues were making their way to the office and, because one of them had not eaten breakfast, they called into a small shop to buy some food. The shopkeeper appeared annoyed and when the hungry friend handed over a banknote for some sandwiches, a drink and a newspaper he just snatched it from the workmate. Then, without even looking at her, slammed the coins down on the counter and shouted, 'Next' to the following customer.

When they had retreated outside the shop, the second friend said, "I'd be really annoyed if I'd been treated that way," to which the first replied, "I will not allow a person like that to decide how I will feel for the rest of the day!"

In other words, we have a choice about how we respond to things which happen to us. Often, in the heat of the moment, we feel that we have no choice but if we stop or slow ourselves down we can choose to respond in another direction. Of course, changing our attitude about something we deeply care is not easy and, in fact, life would lose a lot of its meaning if we didn't invest our emotions in things which are important to us such as our family and friends and even our sports teams.

We have discussed how feelings follow thoughts and if we have sad thoughts then we are likely to feel sad. If we have angry thoughts we will feel angry. If we have happy thoughts we will feel happy. These emotions may have been influenced by others but in some ways we inflict these feelings on ourselves. We have the power and the ability to control our thoughts and therefore our feelings and this degree of control is illustrated by Eleanor Roosevelt who said,

"No one can make you feel inferior, without your permission."

YOUR PERSONAL MOVIE

Our brains have a phenomenal ability to imagine in pictures, in other words to visualize. Think about your home: what colour is your front door? Where is the television? Where do you keep the chocolate cookies? Our brains immediately go to the answer and we don't see these objects as words but as visible things which we picture in our mind's eye.

Can you remember that idyllic holiday you had? Where did you go? Who was there? What did you do? What colour was the sea, sand and sky? We have this wonderful ability to imagine in full colour and to guide the movie to the parts which we like best. We can run and re-run the movie as often as we like and even create different stories and endings.

Not only do we see the images we can also imagine the sounds and voices of people we know including ourselves. If we choose, we can sense what it was like to be there, the touch of another person; the feel of sand between our toes; the warm sea washing against our legs. Our imaginative ability is much better than the movies, we can bask in all the sensory experiences which an ordinary movie is unable to provide. And the reason our personal movies are so special is that our thinking about doing something for real and imagining it are pretty much the same thing because they fire the same parts of the brain. This ability to dream and imagine is a natural one which will improve the more we practice it. Where are your dreams taking you?

THINK YOURSELF BETTER

We regularly change our attention from one thing to another. For example, we might be deeply involved in a TV drama one moment and then the phone rings and we begin chatting with a friend about a completely different subject. Switching our focus is something which we do all the time, often automatically, but we can also do this when we choose. This evidence shows that we are in charge of what we think about although sometimes it may feel that our thoughts are in charge of us!

In recent years there has been an extraordinary growth in the use of cognitive behavioural therapy which, essentially, is about how we think and what we do. In fact, this is nothing new and people have been doing it since at least the time of the Ancient Greeks. For example, the philosopher Epictetus said,

"Men are disturbed not by things, but the view they take of them."

Cognitive behavioural therapy was developed by Aaron Beck who built his therapy on the work of Arthur Ellis. Basically, the foundations of CBT are that we can choose our thoughts; and our thoughts influence our feelings and affect our behaviour. There is a cascade from thoughts to feelings to actions.

The key to how we live our life and how successful we are in the future is how we choose to think about things. Imagine that you pass a friend in the street and they appear to ignore you. You can interpret this situation as meaning that they no longer like you and when you get home you might feel unloved and unhappy. When you next see your friend you might deliberately look the other way and pay them no attention causing them to feel snubbed and thus creating a self-perpetuating negative circle of dislike.

Another way to analyse this situation is to test the accuracy of your interpretation about how your friend appeared. Perhaps they were looking preoccupied and had something important or urgent on their minds. It is probably unlikely that they were intentionally ignoring you and the best thing to do is to make contact and sensitively find out what the true circumstances are. This is the strategy explained by

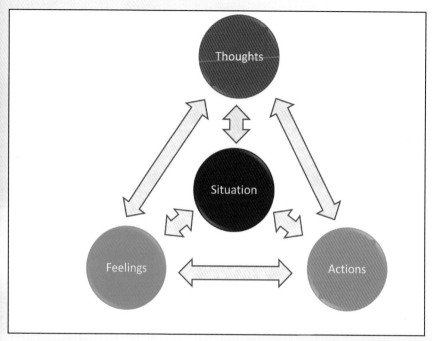

Martin Seligman who suggested that people dispute their thoughts and this is described in the section on Learned Helplessness above.

Cognitive therapy encourages people to test the validity of their thoughts to see if they are accurate and realistic. Sometimes their thoughts are cognitive distortions which can misrepresent actual situations and cause distress and reduce their ability to cope with situations. Examples of these distortions include: mindreading – the example above where people read more into a situation than is reasonable; exaggerating – making a mountain out of a molehill; fortune telling – not going to an event such as a party because people will ignore you and you won't have a good time which becomes a self-fulfilling prophecy; black and white thinking where things are only good or bad; and, labelling people (including themselves) as always having to be successful, always being failures etc.

We don't just talk with other people we also talk to ourselves. In fact, we chatter away to ourselves to such an extent that we can lose track of what is going on all around us. We may not even notice this self-talk but if we monitor our thoughts we will find that these conversations are regularly playing out in our heads. Sometimes these thoughts are very positive and at other times they are the opposite.

Various sections in the book have described how we are not our thoughts and that we can be selective and choose which thoughts on which we wish to concentrate. This gives us an opportunity to monitor what we are thinking and see if it is a balanced view of what really happened, is happening, or might happen. Once we begin to recognise these negative thoughts and self-talk, we can redirect our thinking to more positive aspects of our lives or work to prevent ourselves from wallowing or ruminating about things which make us feel down. We need to learn to recognise and challenge the negative self-talk assumptions which we often have with ourselves. Realism is one thing, talking ourselves down and making ourselves feel unhappy is quite another. Some helpful strategies to analyse self-talk include:

- Take time out to think about thoughts.
- Are they a balanced view of situations?
- Do other people see the same events differently? Why?
- Is my self-talk negative?
- Is this self-talk realistic?
- Might there be different and more constructive ways of thinking about this?
- Do I need to think/worry about this all the time? Can I come back to this later?
- Use distraction to think about something else.
- Taking carefully considered action might resolve the situation.

HABITS SHAPE BEHAVIOURS

When we are learning a new task it is often helpful to talk ourselves through the process. For example, when we were young and learning to tie a knot in our shoelaces we may have mentally talked ourselves through the process, e.g. "Okay, first grab the ends and then cross them over pulling one end through the gap, next... etc."

Over time, the tying of our laces became progressively easier so that eventually we could do it without thinking. A similar thing happens as we get older and learn to swim, ride a bicycle or learn to drive an automobile. At first we can be overwhelmed with the amount of things which we need to pay attention to: steering, shifting gears, looking in the mirrors, paying attention to other road users etc. After an hour's practice we are mentally exhausted and need to rest.

When we are learning something new it takes a lot of our attention and energy to focus on what we would like to achieve. But the more we practice and make the activity a habit the simpler it becomes and less attention and energy are needed to be successful. Eventually, we don't have to use the conscious part of our brains to pay attention because the activity becomes automatic and is controlled by the subconscious part of the brain. The beauty of this is that we can then use our conscious brains to think about other things such as what we want to buy in the store as we are driving there. So the more we carry out an activity the smoother and more professional it becomes. And, as we have discussed, mentally rehearsing something activates the same areas of the brain as physically doing it, so the more we undertake mental practice the better we will become when it actually happens in real life. The reason we get better with practice is that the mental pathways in our brains become more like wide highways which strengthen and speed up the connections. As the Greek philosopher Aristotle said:

"We are what we repeatedly do. Excellence, then, is not an act, but a habit."

MENTAL ESCAPADES

FEELING TRAPPED? ESCAPE INSIDE YOUR HEAD

Our imagination is a wonderfully powerful tool which we can use to escape from the present situation to a fantasy world which we create in our heads. And, the more we use our imagination the better we become at this skill of daydreaming as we saw above.

Sometimes, our work, family or other responsibilities require us to hold back from fulfilling what we would really like to be doing. Sometimes, we have to deal with the present because working pays the bills; or a crying child needs love and attention etc. Sometimes there are jobs which can be extremely monotonous but they can present us with an opportunity to daydream and think of more pleasant activities or things which we would like to achieve. This might involve planning what we want to do at the end of the day when we finish work, or envisaging how to make the most of an upcoming and well-deserved holiday. Likewise, when there is time committed to something such as travelling on a bus, train or airplane there is the opportunity to explore our personal dream landscape.

The important thing to realise is that our brains provide us with a virtual time machine which can transport us to a multiplicity of places and situations and this can provide an outlet when the real world is less than is desired or there is no other opportunity of escape. There are many examples of how people have used their imaginations to escape from their present situations including ones where they have been incarcerated or physically trapped and the following sections present a few examples.

IN A BLINK OF AN EYE

One day Jean-Dominique Bauby suddenly and unexpectedly experienced a severe stroke which placed him in a coma for twenty days. On achieving consciousness he discovered that he was lying in a hospital bed and that much of his body was paralysed and that he was unable to speak. He had 'locked-in syndrome', where the brain continues to operate relatively normally but it does not have any physical control, leaving him helpless and imprisoned inside his own body.

Bauby, aged 43, was a French journalist and editor-in-chief of the French fashion magazine *Elle*. He also had two children and had much to live for but these potential futures were cruelly destroyed by the stroke. He found that the only way he could communicate with people was through blinking his left eyelid.

In spite of his incapacities, Bauby composed a book in his head titled, *The Diving Bell and the Butterfly* and because he was unable to write in his usual way he dictated the book to Claude Mendabil. Slowly and laboriously, Mendabil read the letters of the alphabet and Bauby blinked when he wanted to use a particular letter. It took three hours per day, seven days a week for two months transcribing the book one letter at a time, but eventually the arduous task was completed. Sadly, two days after the book was published Bauby died from pneumonia.

The book was a success and its first print-run sold out on the first day. It was subsequently made into a film which won many awards including a Golden Globe for best foreign film, best director at the Cannes Film Festival, and four Academy Award nominations. But perhaps it is not these physical awards which are Bauby's legacy, rather, he showed us that although our bodies have limited possibilities our minds are free to soar with the birds, swim with the dolphins or visit places on the other side of the world. He compared himself to someone trapped inside a diving bell who can only look at things and not engage directly with things around him but his mind had the ability to fly like a butterfly and he wrote:

> *"There is so much to do. You can wander off in space or in time, set out for Tierra del Fuego or for King Midas's court. You can visit the woman you love, slide down beside her and stroke her still-sleeping face. You can build castles in Spain, steal the Golden Fleece, discover Atlantis, realise your childhood dreams and adult ambitions."*

ANYONE FOR TENNIS?

The power of imagination and dreaming are also proving to be helpful tools for communicating with people who are locked into a coma. Until recently people could remain in a coma for years and it was not known if they would ever recover or if their brains had been irreparably damaged. However, advances in imaging technology have provide a way for some people in comas to communicate to the outside world. When we undertake a physical activity or think about doing that

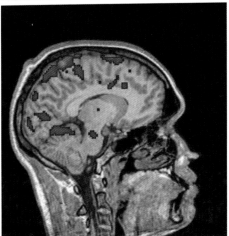

activity the same area of our brains becomes active and as more blood flows to this area sensitive brain scanners can pick up the signals.

Using a brain scanner scientists at Cambridge University discovered that a woman in a persistent vegetative state, as a result of a car accident, was able to understand speech. When sentences were played to her different parts of her brain began to light up and indicated that she understood the words even though she appeared deeply unconscious.

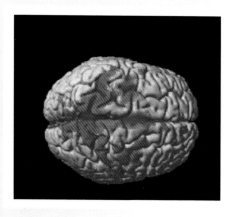

The woman liked tennis and so to test their findings the scientists asked her to imagine playing a big rally on the centre court at Wimbledon. The brain scanner indicated that her brain lit up in the area involved with physical activity. They then asked her to imagine walking around the rooms in her apartment and the brain area associated with mental maps and the geography of space lit up.

This process has now advanced so that the scientists can ask people in a coma to think about playing tennis which means 'Yes', and when they think about the rooms in their home this means 'No.' In this way the patient was able to communicate with the outside world and correctly answered questions about members of his family. This type of mind reading opens up all sorts of possibilities for people who suffer these conditions.

DREAMING IN CAPTIVITY

It is not just when people are physically incapacitated that dreaming provides a means of escape. Aung San Suu Kyi campaigned for democracy in Burma and convincingly won a national election which would have given her political party control but the military junta refused to hand over power. Instead, they placed her under house arrest and in prison several times which added up to fifteen years of detention.

Suu Kyi followed Buddhist teaching and Mahatma Ghandi's philosophy of non-violence which earned her much support from her own people and overseas. As a result, she won the Nobel Peace prize and used the money to fund an education and health trust for the Burmese people.

This enforced captivity was very demanding and during this time she was separated from her children and husband. He became ill, was refused entry to Burma, and later died without seeing his wife for a last time.

Eventually, she regained her freedom and when she was asked how it felt to be released from the house arrest she responded that, "I felt no difference because my mind had always been free."

Suu Kyi has made many speeches which have endeared her to the Burmese people and one for BBC radio described how she managed in captivity – she ended the talk with Rudyard Kipling's poem *The Fairies' Siege*:

> *I'd not give way for an Emperor,*
> *I'd hold my road for a King –*
> *To the Triple Crown I would not bow down –*
> *But this is a different thing.*
> *I'll not fight with the Powers of Air,*
> *Sentry, pass him through!*
> *Drawbridge let fall, 'tis the Lord of us all,*
> *The Dreamer whose dreams come true!*

PLANNING AND MENTAL REHEARSAL

At the age of ten Natascha Kampusch was kidnapped on her way to school in Vienna and bundled into a van. She was then held in a small cellar beneath a garage for eight years and abused by her kidnapper, Wolfgang Priklopil. At the time of her kidnap the police searched extensively but were unable to find her and she was eventually presumed dead.

The cellar where she was held captive was only 5 square metres (54 square feet) and had a concrete door which was hidden by a cupboard. For six months Kampusch did not leave the cellar and then, gradually, she was allowed to spend increasing amounts of time in the house above but was always returned to the cellar at night and when her kidnapper was at work. During this time she educated herself with books which her kidnapper brought her and by listening to the radio.

One day she was outdoors vacuuming her kidnapper's car while he supervised her and when his mobile phone rang he went inside the house to avoid the noise of the vacuum cleaner. Kampusch seized her opportunity and, after running through gardens and climbing fences, banged on a door where the occupant took her in and telephoned the police. On discovering her escape Priklopil jumped in front of a train and killed himself.

Kampusch was reunited with her family and was given much support to enable her to recover from her ordeal. In describing her escape she said that she had spent many years planning how to escape and had rehearsed it many times in her head. When she recognised her opportunity to escape she knew exactly what she would do and successfully escaped after being held captive for 3096 days.

Imprisoned but Free

When times are dark and it is hard to think about our future it can sometimes help to think about tough situations which we have overcome and this can give us confidence. If this is not possible we can take solace in the trials of other people and how they managed and coped with their situations. One example of extreme suffering was that experienced by Viktor Frankl. He was held prisoner in concentration camps during the Second World War and his wife, father and mother perished in the camps.

Although Frankl spent much of his time working as a slave labourer he also used his skills as a doctor and psychiatrist to provide support to depressed inmates and those who had tired of life. When the war ended and he was released, he wrote a book about his experiences and how people might psychologically survive troubling circumstances. The book, *Man's Search for Meaning* sold millions of copies and has been a source of strength for many people.

In the book, Frankl described how, on one occasion, he and many other prisoners were force-marched overnight through desperate icy conditions. As dawn emerged from the darkness Frankl described how:

> *"My mind clung to my wife's image, imagining it with an uncanny acuteness. I heard her answering me, saw her smile, her frank and encouraging look. Real or not, her look was then more luminous than the sun which was beginning to rise."*

This profound experience was a revelation to Frankl who said that "The salvation of man is through love and in love." He owned nothing and had little hope for the future but he still experienced bliss through dreaming about his beloved and he described how he understood for the first time, "The angels are lost in perpetual contemplation of an infinite glory."

Frankl also described how life was so hard for those in the concentration camps that they could barely endure the harshness. What kept many of them going was to live their lives in their heads through dreams and imagination and these were things which the SS did not have the ability to destroy.

It is clear from the situations described above that the ability to dream can free people who are trapped in various situations as Jean-Dominique Bauby, Aung San Suu Kyi, Natascha Kampusch and Viktor Frankl have demonstrated. Hardship taught them how their minds have a wonderful ability to provide virtual freedom and they used this ability to help them survive.

Thoughts can also imprison people unless the mind takes control over them and directs them for a constructive purpose. For example, President Clinton once asked Nelson Mandela, "How do you forgive your jailers?" and Mandela replied:

"When I walked out of the gate I knew that if I continued to hate these people I was still in prison."

CONFIDENCE AND BELIEF

CONFIDENCE

To take control of our lives we need confidence in order to make decisions. Confidence is the belief in oneself and one's abilities to achieve a task. If we possess confidence then we are more likely to undertake an action and that inner belief will often carry us through until it is satisfactorily completed. On the other hand, if we do not have confidence and trust in our abilities then we are less likely to even attempt it. In other words, we have failed before we have even tried!

Confidence in ourselves also inspires confidence in others so how we present ourselves to the world will influence what might happen. If we show confidence people will believe in us. If we show lack of resolve and doubt then people will also doubt us. However, we need to moderate our behaviour, over-confident people tend to become less likeable and so it is important to present a modest appearance.

One of the best ways of preparing for a challenge is to think ahead about how you will cope while it is happening. Talking to yourself is a useful way of managing this and you might say, "This may be difficult, but I am in control, and I will see it through." "I am anxious, which is natural, but there is nothing here that I haven't overcome before."

Confidence is also about believing we can achieve something in the future even though the future is uncertain. We can look backwards and describe what happened but the same does not apply to the future – we may have twenty-twenty hindsight but not twenty-twenty foresight. We have to trust in our abilities to achieve something even though we are not able to look into the future.

Steve Jobs, the late co-founder of Apple Corp, gave a Stanford University Commencement Address in which he emphasised the importance of confidence in personal skills and abilities. He encouraged the graduating students and said:

> *"You can't connect the dots looking forward you can only connect them looking backwards. So you have to trust that the dots will somehow connect in your future. You have to trust in something: your gut, destiny, life, karma, whatever. Because believing that the dots will connect down the road will give you the confidence to follow your heart, even when it leads you off the well-worn path."*

YOU CAN IF YOU THINK YOU CAN

THINKING

If you think you are beaten, you are
If you think you dare not, you don't,
If you like to win, but you think you can't
It is almost certain you won't.

If you think you'll lose, you're lost
For out of the world we find,
Success begins with a fellow's will
It's all in the state of mind.

If you think you are outclassed, you are
You've got to think high to rise,
You've got to be sure of yourself before
You can ever win a prize.

Life's battles don't always go
To the stronger or faster man,
But soon or late the man who wins
Is the man who thinks he can!

WALTER D. WINTLE

DREAM SUMMARIES

We can monitor and direct our thoughts.

We can focus our thoughts and exclude others.

Our thoughts influence our feelings and our feelings influence our thoughts.

Self-talk can inhibit us or encourage us – we can choose.

We can choose the extent to which allow others to influence our feelings.

In some situations our imagination and dreams provide us with escape and hope for the future.

4
FUTURE HORIZONS

"Time is too slow for those who wait, too swift for those who fear, too long for those who grieve, too short for those who rejoice, but for those who love, time is eternity."
HENRY VAN DYKE (1852-1933) US AUTHOR, EDUCATOR AND
CLERGYMAN

INTRODUCTION

For young children even tomorrow appears to be very far away especially if there is the promise of a reward or a treat. As we get older our time horizons tend to expand and influence our behaviour as we learn that the actions of today have consequences for tomorrow. It appears that if we can restrain our needs now this mental toughness may well help us achieve more life success in the future.

Having expectations about ourselves and others can affect performance as we saw with the self-fulfilling prophecy in Chapter 1 and in this chapter we will explore how our dreams about our futures can influence our careers and what we can achieve in life.

HOW FAR CAN YOU SEE INTO THE FUTURE?

TIME HORIZONS FOR THE YOUNG AND OLD

When we stand on a beach close to the sea the horizon appears only a few miles distant but if we stand on a cliff and look out over the waters the horizon recedes further into the distance. This is why in the days of sailing ships a sailor was sent to climb to the top of the mast and spy out what could not be seen from the decks below.

In a similar way, age provides us with a longer perspective on time. The more experience we have the more we can assess and evaluate how we can use our time. We may also have a greater recognition that our time is limited and therefore value it more thus taking opportunities when they arise.

Can you remember when you were young and waiting for birthdays, Christmas and other holidays that seemed to take forever to arrive.

They appeared so far into the future that it was not even possible to understand this extended concept of time. Young children very much live in the present and as they grow older their understanding of time gradually extends and they appreciate the concept better.

But time is an elusive concept which increases in complexity the more we try to examine it. And, our perception of time varies, for example Albert Einstein said:

"When a man sits with a pretty girl for an hour, it seems like a minute. But let him sit on a hot stove for a minute and it's longer than any hour. That's relativity."

And time is valuable. People frequently squander time because they feel that there is an almost unlimited supply of it when, in fact, the amount we are allocated is restricted. Indeed, time is sometimes more valuable than money since we can get more money but we cannot get more time. This dilemma between time and money is a common one – we will often spend money to make more time e.g. taking and paying for a taxi when we are in a hurry.

How near or far is your personal time horizon and how much do you want to squeeze into this space? Time passes the same for everyone but some people achieve a lot and others a little. How much do you want to achieve?

THE MARSHMALLOW EFFECT

Are you one of those people who can't function without a mug of fresh coffee or tea in the morning? Or perhaps you are one of those people who can't resist the temptation of chocolate. There is nothing inherently wrong with succumbing to the allure of these wonderful temptations but how good are you at resisting them? If you find resisting a cup of coffee a challenge, imagine how much more of an ordeal it is for a young child to ignore a tasty marshmallow placed in front of them while they sit at a table.

This scenario was played out in Bing Nursery School at Stanford University during the late 1960s, where four-year-old children were left alone in a room containing few distractions other than a single marshmallow lying on the table directly in reach. The children were told that if they could avoid eating it for 15 minutes they would be given a second marshmallow. Film of the children shows them struggling to avoid the allure of the candy by covering their eyes, playing with their pigtails, or even stroking the marshmallow. The outcome of this experiment was that two-thirds of the children eventually gave in and

ate the marshmallow. The others who managed to resist the temptation were rewarded with a second marshmallow.

As the years passed, Walter Mischel who ran the experiment and whose three daughters took part in the experiment at the nursery, would occasionally ask them how their friends were getting on at school. The responses varied, but what got Mischel's attention was that those children who were doing well were also the ones who had been able to wait and be rewarded with the second marshmallow.

The feedback from his daughters seemed more than just anecdotal observations and Mischel contacted many of the original six hundred and fifty-three children who were involved with the task together with their parents and teachers. He enquired about how they could think ahead and plan; what their SAT scores were; how they managed problems; and how they got along with the school friends and peers.

The research found that those children who were low delayers were more likely to experience behavioural problems, had lower attention spans, had fewer friendships and had a SAT score of 210 points below those children who could wait 15 minutes for a marshmallow.

It appears that self-discipline can have a major impact on performance and if you are patient and willing to wait for your objective then you may be more successful. This perhaps explains why some people want that new gadget now and others will wait until it has a reduced price in the sales. Most dreams are long term objectives and those with patience are more likely to delay gratification so that the rewards later will be greater.

FUTURES NEAR AND FAR

How often have you promised to: accept an invitation; do something; or go somewhere in the future and then realised when it came near that you really did not have the time or did not want to do it. It would appear that it is much easier for us to commit to something in the distant future even though we would decline the opportunity if it were tomorrow. It seems we believe the future holds much more time than we have in the present and that there is an almost infinite amount of time and opportunity in which we can easily squeeze in that additional request and demand on our time.

People who organize meetings, events and so on often recognise this misperception of time and that is why they carefully organize things well in advance and gain commitment. Once there is this obligation attendees then find it very difficult to excuse themselves even though they may prefer to be somewhere else. One of the best ways of handling these situations is to ask ourselves would we still do it if it were to happen tomorrow or in the near future. If our answer is 'Yes' then we should go ahead. If the answer is 'No' then we should probably decline the offer.

Yet, there is a benefit from committing to things in the future. The obligation of committing to an appointment means that we sometimes take part in things we would not otherwise choose to do in the present time. This can get us out of a rut because when things are in the distant future they do not seem so scary. Since they look far away and appear very small and insignificant this increases our confidence that we can cope with them.

DREAM COOKING

Children can be particularly difficult when being given food and to get them to eat nutritious things often requires us to influence their expectations. If they think it will taste nasty and horrible it probably will; and, if they think it will be yummy and see everyone else enjoying it they will probably love it too.

Children are not alone in their interpretations and expectations about food, so too are adults. Which would you prefer: organic Wensleydale cheese gently melting over a round of lightly toasted home-baked wholemeal bread? Or, a slice of cheese on toast?

Most people would prefer the former because it stimulates their senses and makes their mouths water much more in anticipation than the thought of someone just throwing a plate of cheese on toast in front of them. In fact, the two may be exactly the same but it is the more positively described one which captures their taste buds.

This is why many restaurants and cafés have taken to giving more artistic descriptions of their meals rather than a brief list of the contents. If we expect something to taste good there is a greater likelihood that we will believe it to taste better.

The same is true of the Pepsi Challenge. Many people taking part in a blind tasting of Pepsi preferred it to Coca-Cola. However, when the brands were clearly visible more people preferred Coca-Cola to Pepsi. The reason for this was that because they expected Coca-Cola to taste better they actually believed it tasted better.

So the message is clear. If you want children to eat more healthily and you want to be the perfect host to your dinner guests, then carefully describe what they are going to receive. And carefully present food on fine china plates and drinks in quality crystal glasses, their eyes and your presentation will raise expectations and increase their enjoyment.

EDUCATION FOR ALL

STIMULATE YOUR MIND

Research has discovered that the brains of rats and mice which live in boring or stimulating environments are different. Those which live in stimulating and varied environments are much more developed and have more neural connections than those which lived in very boring and monotonous environments.

And it is not just animals which need sensory stimulation, children living in impoverished situations with few stimulating activities etc. do not develop as much as those who live in situations which are full of challenging and exciting ones. By stimulating their minds, their brains develop and so increase their capabilities to do more and experience more.

However, all environments need to change regularly if they are not to become unnoticed and boring. If we see or hear things on a regular basis we gradually cease to notice that they are there. For example, frequently going from one room to another in our homes or taking a routine journey to work soon become automatic and as we travel we are thinking about other things rather than what is immediately around us. This process of becoming very familiar with things and then not noticing them is called habituation.

Our brains seek out variety because they do not like boredom and it is this sensory deprivation that prisoners so hate when they do not have their freedom. So we should stimulate our brains and continually encourage ourselves to try new things, go to new places, listen to new music, eat new foods etc. We can literally grow our brains.

EDUCATION, EDUCATION, EDUCATION

Children possess an enormous capacity to take in new information and ideas because their brains are very plastic and flexible which means that they have the ability to learn and absorb things very rapidly. For example, adults may find it challenging to learn a new language but if a child is taken to another country and just interacts with other children they will soon learn the language like a native.

This ability to absorb and learn by children should be supported as much as possible. They should be encouraged to try out new things, be exposed to new situations and challenge themselves etc. Dropping them in the deep end is probably not a good idea but slow and increasing exposure will gradually build up their confidence.

Much education is designed not so much for the present but to enhance children's and adults' abilities in the future. Education provides a firm foundation for the future and enables people to draw upon solid principles which will enable them to live happier, healthier and more productive lives. As Euripedes, Phrixus (484BC – 406BC), the Greek dramatist said:

"Who so neglects learning in his youth, loses the past and is dead to the future."

The challenge for many teachers and trainers is to get those reluctant children and adults to engage with the education and training. The problem is that some children and adults prefer to live more in the present and cannot see the benefits of sacrificing their time now for something in the distant future. But, as we saw with the marshmallow experiment those who can control their immediate desires in exchange for higher rewards in the future tend to be happier, healthier and more successful.

We cannot accurately predict what will happen to us in the future but if we give ourselves a good education we will be more prepared to handle what we encounter. For this reason we need to encourage children to dream more vividly about their futures and the things which they can accomplish.

If you are planning for a year plant crops.
If you are planning for a decade plant trees.
If you are planning for a lifetime educate people.
CHINESE PROVERB

CHILDREN'S IMAGINATION

The power of imagination is especially strong in children; so strong sometimes that they are not always able to distinguish between fact and fantasy. And this remarkable ability to visualize while playing enables children to rehearse their skills and thoughts in a safe environment before venturing out into the real world where lessons are sometimes learned in harder ways.

The use of imagination enables children to project their ideas into the future and test their viability. It also allows them to develop their powers of creativity which will help in problem solving and dealing with the challenges which life throws at them.

Those who have seen a child receive a gift and then discard it and play happily with the box instead will understand the power of their imagination. The children's author, Alison Uttley, described how children will make use of anything they find around them to play with and to create a make-believe world:

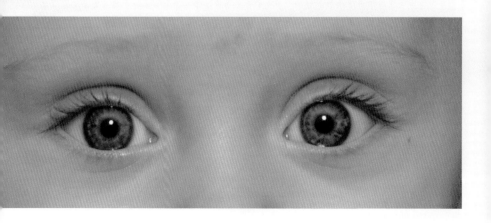

*"The fields were our toyshops and sweetshops, our market and our
storehouses. We made toys from things we found in the pastures.
We ate sweet and sour food of the wild. We hunted from hedge to
hedge as in a market, to find the best provisions, and we had our
wild shops in corners of fields, or among
the trees."*

This ability to imagine and dream in children should be strongly
encouraged so that they learn how to organize information; reflect
on things; develop their concentration; reduce their fear and anxiety;
increase their ability to empathise with other people and increase their social skills. Developing the power to dream and imagine among children and combining this with learning and education will help them to grow into well-balanced and stable adults. It was Joseph Joubert the French writer (1754 – 1824) who noted:

*"He who has imagination
without learning has wings
but no feet."*

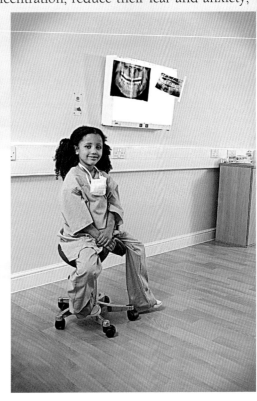

DREAM BIGGER DREAMS

More money is spent on education and training by governments, agencies and individuals than almost anything else in the world. And, the main reason for this is not necessarily for immediate gain although it can be great fun and very satisfying to learn. Instead, it is for the future benefits which will accrue to the educated person and the educated population in the future. An educated person is more likely to be economically successful, healthier and live longer. An educated population will be more productive and so create more wealth to build hospitals, provide social care for the needy, and educate more children and young people thus continuing this positive economic cycle.

Pupils in schools often ask, "Why do we have to do this?" and the answer which often comes from the teacher is, "It will help you get a better job" or something along these lines. The teacher is often akin to a salesperson promoting the idea of a happier and more successful future which is difficult when children and young people have very near time horizons. Inspiring children and their parents that they can achieve their dreams can begin at any stage of their lives but the earlier this happens the better the chance that they will get that dream job etc.

Schools, colleges, universities and centres for education and training are designed to support learning which will benefit all those who attend. Yet, many children from disadvantaged backgrounds tend to have lower personal expectations and therefore don't think of going to college or university. So, for this reason The University of Sheffield recognised the importance of encouraging and inspiring young people to look ahead and imagine what they might become e.g. a dentist, scientist, lawyer or even an astronaut. To do this, photographs were taken of children wearing the oversized work clothes of professional people which were then displayed on banners and other media. This campaign has been very successful in encouraging children to expand their horizons and is called, *Dream Bigger Dreams*. Dreaming of future careers can be highly motivating for many people and Fred Van Amburgh (1866-1944) an author and publisher declared:

"Dream big dreams, then put on your overalls and go out and make the dreams come true."

IMAGINATION LIBRARY

Dolly Parton, the American country singer and actress, grew up in a family of twelve children and lived in a 'dirt poor' one-room cabin in Tennessee. Despite her success she didn't forget her origins and in 1996 launched her *Imagination Library* in her home state. The idea behind the library is to encourage the love of reading among pre-school children and to help them enjoy the magic which is sparked in their imaginations. In this way they learn to love reading and education and so improve their life chances.

Each month specially chosen and age-appropriate books are mailed directly to the children no matter what their family income. Since its launch, the *Imagination Library* has spread across the USA; and been implemented in Canada and the UK. More than 1600 local communities support the project and approximately 700,000 children receive a book each month.

"Listen carefully, then I'll begin," is the way much children's storytelling begins and its purpose is to quieten them, get attention and to encourage their imagination. Dolly Parton's dream of encouraging young children to develop a love of reading, and thus educate and lift themselves from poverty, has transformed lives.

Reading is a wonderful way for developing a child's imagination because they have to mentally engage with the words and create a picture inside their heads. Research has shown that reading also increases the strength of the connections between the two hemispheres of the brain.

Reading and storytelling also act as beneficial forms of rehearsal not only for children but also adults. And, many of the old fairy tales raise awareness of the potential dangers of venturing into the forests and of strangers. In this way children can be warned in advance through cautionary stories about how to handle or avoid potentially dangerous situations. Storytelling and imagination provide a means of running a range of cost-free experiments about future life situations.

Dolly Parton described how when she was growing up she knew that her dreams of becoming a singer would come true. She also recognised that children everywhere have their own dreams of becoming doctors, inventors, ministers, and perhaps singers, and said:

"The seeds of these dreams are often found in books and the seeds you help plant in your community can grow across the world."

FUTURE TALK

Giving people the confidence to dream a different world for themselves is an important step in bringing about change, and one way to help this process is to use a visualisation strategy called future talk. This technique encourages people to imagine themselves in the near future coping with a task which they are presently having difficulty achieving.

96

It is well-known that changing behaviour such as stopping smoking or changing a diet is often difficult to achieve even when people sincerely want to change. And, future talk can be used to put people in a constructive frame of mind to help them reach their objective. The future talk process involves one or more people and frequently uses the following process:

- Imagine you meet a friend next week and that you are doing fine in coping with the task which you currently find difficult.
- Describe to your friend what you 'are' doing and the things which are different to the present time.
- How are you managing and controlling things 'now'?
- When you feel frustrated what are the coping mechanisms which you use?
- Describe the behaviour of other people around you.
- What are they doing that is different?
- Now, in real time, begin doing the things which you imagined yourself doing next week.

Encouraging someone to imagine themselves doing something successfully not only increases their confidence but it also strengthens the cognitive connections in the brain thus making the coping strategies easier to access and achieve. The more a person mentally practices something in their heads the greater the chance they will do it. In other words, we have to dream it to do it.

FANTASIES CAN BECOME REAL

DREAM FANTASIES

The thoughts of many people are often occupied with dreaming about the potential attributes and personality of their ideal partner. Indeed, this is a very helpful way of preparing us to identify those people who match our mental template and it helps us focus our efforts rather than blindly accepting whoever comes along.

When we dream of being with someone we like this releases hormones which make us feel good. This is still the case even if we are not actually involved with the person and sometimes when they are not available our imaginations may be the only source of comfort. Indeed, a dream world is often much better than reality and it can also be a safer alternative when we should not become involved with that person for whatever reason.

People have the mental ability to dream whatever fantasy world they choose and this can be a creative and stimulating experience. Throughout this book we describe the benefits of daydreams and how they can be translated into action. However, there is also a danger that people can become lost in this fantasy world and retreat from the reality. This is probably acceptable for short periods of time but when it becomes obsessive then that is the time to return and live in the real world. Also, dream worlds have a habit of colliding with hard concrete reality and the outcomes may be worse than if a person had faced up to the truth.

The books, *The Secret Life of Walter Mitty* by James Thurber and *Billy Liar* by Keith Waterhouse both describe characters who became lost in their own worlds far removed from reality. Like them, we all spend a great amount of time in fantasy land and we should enjoy these virtual journeys but we should also keep our feet firmly anchored to the ground.

The cartoon characters Calvin and Hobbes described the benefits of dreams when people are distanced from one another. When dreams are shared and people inhabit each other's dreams then they can always be together even when they are far apart. And, this scenario is clearly illustrated below in the story about Pierre and Marie Curie.

Love's Young Dream

Oh! the days are gone when Beauty bright
My heart's chain wove,
When my dream of life from morn till night
Was love, still love.
New hope may bloom,
And days may come
Of milder, calmer beam,
But there's nothing half so sweet in life
As love's young dream:
No, there's nothing half so sweet in life
As love's young dream.
Tho' the bard to purer fame may soar,
When wild youth's past;
Tho' he win the wise, who frown'd before,
To smile at last;
He'll never meet
A joy so sweet,
In all his noon of fame,
As when first he sung to woman's ear
His soul-felt flame,
And, at every close, she blush'd to hear
The one lov'd name!
No, -- that hallow'd form is ne'er forgot
Which first love trac'd!
Still it lingering haunts the greenest spot
Of memory's waste.
'Twas odour fled
As soon as shed:
'Twas morning's wingéd dream:
'Twas a light, that ne'er can shine again
On life's dull stream!
Oh! 'twas light that ne'er can shine again
On life's dull stream!

THOMAS MOORE (1779-1852) IRISH POET

RADIANT DREAMS

Maria Sklodowska was a young woman who left her native Poland to study physics at the University of Paris. Uprooting herself was stressful but this was eased by her sister who lived in Paris and who provided Maria with temporary accommodation and financial support throughout her studies. This gesture reciprocated the earlier generosity of Maria who had used the money she earned as a governess to financially support her sister while she was studying medicine.

On completing her physics degree, Maria then worked in an industrial laboratory and continued to study at the university where she was awarded another degree in mathematics. It was during this time that she met Pierre Curie, a teacher at the School of Physics and Chemistry, and their common interest in magnetism caused a mutual attraction.

Although Maria had grown close to Pierre she still harboured plans to return to Poland and in the summer she travelled to Warsaw. She hoped to find a job which matched her high qualifications but was rejected by Krakow University because she was a woman. During this period, Marie (as she then called herself) and Pierre continued their courtship through long letters with Pierre setting out his thoughts for the future. In one such letter he enticingly wrote,

"It would be a beautiful thing, a thing I dare not hope, if we could spend our life near each other hypnotized by our dreams: your patriotic dream, our humanitarian dream and our scientific dream."

The letters were successful in drawing Marie back to Paris where she and Pierre immersed themselves in research working side by side in the laboratories and a year later they were married. Their explorations were successful and they identified the existence of a new element which was called Polonium after Marie's homeland. Subsequently they discovered the element radium and coined the term radioactivity.

In 1903, Marie, Pierre and Henri Becquerel were awarded the Nobel Prize in Physics by the Royal Swedish Academy of Sciences for their research into the new subject of radiation. Eight years later she was honoured again by the award of the Nobel Prize in Chemistry and was the first person receive two Nobel prizes.

During the Great War, Marie encouraged the use of mobile x-ray vehicles to help in the diagnosis of injured soldiers and these radiography trucks became known as 'Petits-Curies' or 'Little Curies'.

Unfortunately, although the research which Marie and Pierre had conducted was of incalculable value to humanity it was not without cost to their own health. At the time it was not realised that the substances they were researching could damage their health. The research which both Pierre and Marie Curie conducted was done without any of the normal safety precautions which would now be used for dangerous substances. They often carried around the materials in their pockets and stored them in their desks. Gradually, the radioactivity blighted their lives and caused a number of side-effects.

The impact of the research has benefitted people since and many awards and institutions have been named after the pair. A unit of radioactivity has been named a 'curie' and Marie was named the "most inspirational woman in science" by *New Scientist* magazine. There are even Marie Curie Cancer Care and Research funds which support investigation into a cure for this disease and which provide nursing care for ill people.

The letter Pierre wrote enticing Marie back to Paris by describing the possibilities of achieving their dreams achieved its objectives. He won the heart of the woman he loved and together they pushed forward the frontiers of science. Perhaps all of these discoveries and achievements might not have happened without the dreams of Marie and Pierre Curie.

THE FUTURES

We often use the term 'the future' which suggests that there is only one future which we are heading towards. Yet, the future is not a concrete thing and does not really exist except in our heads. In fact, there are many possible futures which is why our minds spend so much time pondering what we might do. We think about what we are going to eat in the evening; what we are going to do at the weekend; how we might spend the rest of our lives etc.

The reality is that there is no 'the future' and we should carefully monitor our thinking when we use this term. If we narrow our thinking to just one option we might miss other opportunities because we do not allow ourselves to think about them. There is nothing wrong with deciding on a particular future the important thing is that we have carefully considered other possibilities first.

So when someone says, "The future will be X", we should closely examine what assumptions are being made when they suggest that there is only one destination. It is possible that there are other destinations and that they have not been properly investigated. Even if a particular destination or point on the horizon is chosen, there may be many avenues which will get us there. For example, we may decide to study a particular subject at college or university, do we do it now or wait until we have more time; which college or university do we wish to study at; are we going to do it full-time or part-time? There are many possibilities and our task is to weigh them and make a calculated decision.

DREAM SUMMARIES

- Young children live very much in the present and have near time horizons.

- As people grow older they develop a longer perspective on time.

- Those people who have self-control and can defer immediate gratification tend to be more successful in their lives.

- Education and reading stimulate the abilities of children and adults to dream.

- Imagining the possible outcomes of different decisions enables people to weigh up the best course of action.

- Fantasies are very alluring but should be carefully balanced with living in the real world.

5
DREAMS AT WORK

"All men dream: but not equally. Those who dream by night in the dusty recesses of their minds wake in the day to find that it was vanity: but the dreamers of the day are dangerous men, for they may act their dreams with open eyes, to make it possible."
T. E. LAWRENCE (1888-1935) LAWRENCE OF ARABIA, AUTHOR.

INTRODUCTION

Dreams are free yet our ability to achieve them depends on how realistic they are, our energy and our motivation. Yet there are some people whose dreams seem to inspire not just themselves but the people around them, for example, Martin Luther King Jr. dreamed of a world where people would have the same opportunities whatever background they came from.

Yet, the future is very unclear and even the fortune teller's crystal ball provides little guidance for us. This lack of clarity is largely due to the fact that even small changes can cause a big impact; just a slight deviation along a pathway can lead to unanticipated encounters with new opportunities and challenges. And this is one of the reasons why it is so hard to provide an accurate weather forecast or even predict which way the stock market will go.

Whether we recognise it or not our lives are always at a cross-roads. Think about how politicians, our bosses, family and friends can swiftly alter the direction of our lives. All it needs is one event to turn our life upside-down in a positive or negative way. If just one of these many factors happens it can change our lives, for instance, meeting someone, seeing a job advert that is perfectly matched for us, spotting that dream home etc. But dreaming and thinking about the future can help us increase our luck and open up new opportunities which we would never have noticed if we had not dreamed in the first place. This chapter will explore the uncertainty of the future but also how we can increase our luck in love and life. It will also describe examples of people who dared to dream and realise their dreams. And, as we explained, dreams are free and are often the best way of identifying a solution to our problems which saves us money. It was Ernest Rutherford the Nobel laureate who said:

"Gentlemen, we have run out of money. It is time to start thinking."

Uncertain Futures

The Plans of Mice and Men

We can plan, and we can scheme, and we can invest all our energies in trying to create our envisioned future but sometimes it is to no avail. This failure to achieve what we want is not always a result of our shortcomings and ability to predict. Rather, it is the fact that it is impossible to foresee everything which might affect us, and sometimes these rare or unpredictable events have the ability to blow us of course.

Robert Burns, the Scottish poet, was well aware of the capricious forces which can suddenly and seriously change our lives. Although he was a respected poet he needed to supplement his income by farming which is why he is also known as the 'Ploughman Bard'. One day while ploughing a field he overturned a mouse's nest causing it to run away. The nest which the mouse had built with leaves and wheat stubble was designed to withstand the severe freezing winters, and it was suddenly destroyed and the mouse was harshly evicted.

Burns felt much sympathy for the mouse as a fellow traveller through life since it had been minding its own business and harming no one except for eating the occasional ear of wheat, which the ploughman would not miss. Burns drew parallels with the human predicament and the fact that we, too, can have our carefully organized plans devastated by overpowering forces. To symbolise this Burns wrote his 1785 poem 'To A Mouse' and said:

> But Mouse, you are not alone,
> In proving foresight may be vain:
> The best laid schemes of mice and men
> Go often askew,
> And leaves us nothing but grief and pain,
> For promised joy!

This warning from Burns conveys a powerful message, and one which we should carefully bear in mind. Sometimes it may be necessary to have a Plan B, a fall-back strategy which will allow us to continue with an alternative option. In this way the chances of both plans being badly affected by unpredictable external conditions is far less and thus allows us to relax a little and continue our lives.

BUTTERFLIES AND THE WEATHER

Have you ever checked the weather forecast to see that it promised to be a beautiful day and left home wearing only light clothing? Only later, when you were soaked to the skin did you think: "I should have carried an umbrella." It is easy to blame the weather forecasters but, most likely, they will also have been following their own predictions and have got drenched as well.

To increase the accuracy of weather forecasts larger volumes of meteorological information were collected by ground stations, satellites, and sensors located in the seas and oceans. And, as greater amounts of information poured in it became more difficult to process it thus requiring bigger and more advanced computers. It was thought that more powerful computers would provide a significant improvement in the accuracy of the forecasts. Yet the accuracy of the weather forecasts for more than a few days ahead barely changed!

The reason for this failure to provide accurate weather forecasts was eventually deciphered by Edward Lorenz who conducted research using computers-models of the weather. On one occasion he repeated an experiment and, to save time, fed data into the computer using rounded numbers which had small fractions removed. This second running of the figures produced a startlingly different weather prediction to the first run. Lorenz concluded that even very small changes could result, over the longer term, in completely different weather. He suggested that the flapping of a butterfly's wings in Brazil might set off a tornado in Texas and so chaos theory became known as the 'butterfly effect'.

We can see this butterfly effect in many different places. Imagine holding a pile of dry sand between your hands and slowly releasing your grip so that it slowly falls out creating a cone. As the cone increases in size it will occasionally collapse when the steepness of the slope becomes too great. As more sand is added the cone will build up until, once again, it collapses. Essentially, it might take just one grain of sand to tip the balance and cause the mini-avalanche. Indeed, rock and snow avalanches can be triggered by minute changes such as someone skiing over the area particularly if the slope's gradient is 38 degrees or more.

So what are the messages we can learn from the butterfly effect? Well, it can mean that with just a little more effort we can overcome those things which are holding us back from achieving our plans. Just one person can achieve astonishing things if they put their minds to it. After all, if the apparently fragile Monarch butterfly can make its way from the forests of Mexico all the way to Canada and back, what we can first dream of and then achieve?

IF ONLY AND WHAT IF?

Our minds are time machines which allow us to go back in time and explore those 'if only' situations and also go forward into the future to ask 'what if' questions. Mentally travelling back to a significant junction in our lives such as a job offer or invitation on a date, provides us with the opportunity to reassess how we might have handled it differently and taken another route. Unfortunately, we cannot turn back the clock although there are some circumstances and opportunities which can return. The main benefit of revisiting these events is so that we can learn from them and thus minimise the chances of us making the wrong choice in the future.

Our minds are also designed to time-travel into the future by asking ourselves 'What if?' questions which help us to explore the various possibilities and make a judgment about which avenue to go down. We spend much of our waking lives thinking about what we are going to do and assessing the potential outcomes of our actions e.g. "What if I buy that house; is it a good investment?"

It is this ability to think about the consequences of future actions which has the potential to provide us with big advantages. If you can explore and examine the future better than other people this will give you an edge. You will have a more reasoned insight into whether to take action or hold back until the time is more suitable.

Asking ourselves, 'What if' questions is a much safer way of assessing our options. If we did not have this ability we would always have to do things physically in order to find out what would happen. This of course can be quite dangerous e.g. imagine standing on a cliff edge and not knowing if it was dangerous or not to jump?

LEARNING FROM THE FUTURE

This ability for mental time-travel enables us to learn from the future and avoid making actual physical mistakes. The term 'scrooge', describes a mean, miserly person and originated from Charles Dickens' story *A Christmas Carol* about an unpleasant employer called Ebenezer Scrooge. One night just before Christmas, Scrooge is visited in his bedroom by the ghost of his old business partner Jacob Marley who then tells Scrooge to change his ways. Three further ghosts visit Scrooge, the first, The Ghost of Christmas Past, shows Scrooge in his younger days enjoying life.

The second ghost, The Ghost of Christmas Present, takes Scrooge to see the home of his employee Bob Cratchit who cannot afford a proper

Christmas dinner. It is also made clear that Bob cannot afford the medical treatment to help his sick son, Tiny Tim, because Scrooge pays such poor wages.

The third and final ghost, The Ghost of Christmas Yet to Come, warns Scrooge about what will happen if he does not change his ways. One of the things that will happen in the future is the death of Tiny Tim and Scrooge is deeply saddened and affected by the scenes which the ghost revealed.

> *"Ghost of the Future," he exclaimed, "I fear you more than any spectre I have seen. But as I know your purpose is to do me good, and as I hope to live to be another man from what I was, I am prepared to bear you company, and do it with a thankful heart. Will you not speak to me?"*

> *"Men's courses will foreshadow certain ends, to which, if persevered in, they must lead," said Scrooge. "But if the courses be departed from, the ends will change. Say it is thus with what you show me."*

Scrooge does change his behaviour and Tiny Tim's life is spared, and Scrooge's message is a powerful one which reminds us that the future is not preordained and can be influenced if we change our behaviour now. We know that certain behaviours will produce specific consequences and if these are not desirable ones then we need to change our behaviours. If we can dream of a different future then we can work towards it.

I HAVE A DREAM

One of the reasons why we dream is to envision a better life for ourselves or for others. It is part of the human condition to strive to improve ourselves and this picturing of better circumstances is a natural first step on the journey to make things happen. Mostly, our dreams are on a small scale and involve only ourselves and those close to us. But, there are some people who have dreams which are much larger than just a better life for themselves and their families. Sometimes they dream of changing their whole community, or their whole country, or the whole world. One of these dreamers was Martin Luther King Jr. who dreamed of replacing the discriminatory laws in the United States which segregated black people and restricted many aspects of their everyday life including shopping and travelling.

King, the son of a minister, was born in 1929 in Atlanta, Georgia. He was ambitious and skipped the ninth and twelfth grades at school, went to college at fifteen and graduated with a degree at the young age of only nineteen. He then attended a theological seminary, studied for another degree and subsequently became a Baptist minister in Montgomery, Alabama.

In 1959, King travelled to India and visited the birthplace of Mahatma Gandhi who had led the campaign for Indian independence through non-violent civil disobedience. Inspired by his visit King returned home and campaigned for equal civil rights through peaceful means.

One of the defining moments in the campaign happened in 1955 when Rosa Parks and three other black people were asked by the bus driver to give up their seats to allow white passengers to sit down. Only Parks refused the driver's request and so he called the police who arrested her for violating the local segregation laws. She went to trial four days later and was fined $10 plus $4 court costs. However, she appealed the ruling and challenged the legality of the local laws.

On the day of the trial a boycott of the buses was organized by the black community and led by King. A further boycott which called for the ending of segregation and a request for black drivers to be employed by the bus company lasted for more than a year until the segregation laws were repealed. During this time King was arrested and also had his home bombed. King was galvanised to continue actions aimed at ending the unfair segregation laws which included public schooling and voting restrictions which discriminated against the black community. He supported numerous other campaigns and in 1963 civil rights organisations organized what was then the largest march and rally to be held at the Lincoln Memorial in Washington DC. The March on Washington for Jobs and Freedom was where King made his famous 'I have a dream speech'.

In his speech King described the difficulties which black Americans faced in their everyday lives and drew on the enduring words of Thomas Jefferson in the *Declaration of Independence* which proclaimed:

> *"We hold these truths to be self-evident, that all men are created equal, that they endowed by their Creator with certain unalienable Rights, that among these are Life, Liberty and the pursuit of Happiness."*

King painted a picture of people from all backgrounds living harmoniously together and gave the crowd hope and inspiration to return to their communities and campaign for a free, fair and just society in which all people were created equal. In spite of the challenges and obstacles which existed King said:

> *"I still have a dream. It is a dream deeply rooted in the American dream."*

The power of his oratory and the passionate delivery of the Dream speech moved people from all backgrounds to support equal rights and in 1964 the Civil Rights Act was passed and it also included equal employment rights for women. In the same year King was awarded the Nobel Peace Prize.

King's beliefs and hopes for the future didn't go down well with everyone and in 1968 he was assassinated. This ended his physical involvement with civil rights but it was not the end of his dream because it continues to inspire countless people to support the cause of civil rights to this day. This influence is demonstrated by the Martin Luther King Junior Day which is a national holiday in the United States.

DREAMS OF WEALTH

ANTICIPATION AND PREVENTION

It is well-known that young and inexperienced drivers are more likely to have accidents and sixteen-year-old drivers are eight times more likely to be involved in an accident than those aged between 45-64. In some ways we might find this surprising because their coordination is generally better, their reactions are faster, and their eyesight is sharper than their elders. However, young and inexperienced drivers not only tend to take greater risks they also lack the experience to recognise potential trouble spots and instead keep their eyes on the road ahead in order to stay in lane.

Older drivers with more experience know the roads better, have seen more challenging situations and often know how to respond in a safe manner. Also, research into the eye movements of experienced drivers shows that their eyes are continuously darting around looking for potential problems. They don't know that something will happen but they focus their attention on known trouble spots where danger may lie.

Similarly, parents supervising young children know all too well that it is good to keep an eye on them and when the youngsters start to move towards a hot stove etc. the parents quickly lift them to safety or steer them away from danger. The parents are not predicting what will happen but they are anticipating that their children may place themselves in harm's way.

This anticipatory thinking is often based on experiences whether good, bad or indifferent. If we have had positive experiences where things have gone smoothly we remember them and repeat that same behaviour to increase our chances of success. If, on the other hand, things went wrong we will try to avoid repeating the things we did the last time e.g. losing concentration in a meeting or presentation. Using our past experience to help us anticipate the future is a well-founded basis to achieve our dreams. As Winston Churchill said:

"The further backward you look, the further forward you can see."

ANTICIPATE TO ACCUMULATE

One of the biggest problems during the Credit Crunch crisis was that many of the traders were young and had never experienced a downturn in the markets. Their mindset was that things would continue in a positive way and because almost everyone else was thinking in the same way they did not deeply consider what might happen and continued to make dangerous trades. Eventually, as we all know, this wishful thinking combined with mistakes unravelled and caused enormous social and economic damage.

Sensibly managing our personal finances requires us think beyond the immediate demands of today. Do we have enough money put away to pay for that large bill next month? For example, did spending a lot of money during the last holiday mean that, later, when the bills arrived there wasn't enough to pay them all? This might have meant taking a loan at a high interest rate resulting in even more money being paid back.

If we look ahead and budget carefully by anticipating how much we need over the year rather than the next few days we are going to be in a much more comfortable situation. Knowing that the price of certain things goes up at certain times of the year should encourage us to plan our visits to the store more carefully. If we can't afford something today it is probable that we can't afford it tomorrow – don't store up financial problems by taking on loans which transfer today's problems until tomorrow.

Many people look much further ahead by saving for their retirement and ensuring that they have a pension which will give them a reasonable standard of living in their old age. Retirement may seem distant but small savings now accumulate into larger sums over the longer term and can make the difference between a comfortable old age and one spent scrimping and saving because there is not enough for our needs. Being farsighted doesn't just mean having good eyesight, it means preparing now for our dreams of the future.

THINK AND GROW RICH

Andrew Carnegie, the successful steel industrialist, was so impressed during an interview by the local reporter, Napoleon Hill, that he commissioned Hill to interview 500 successful people and discover what made them successful. During this process Hill interviewed a range of successful business people and politicians including: Alexander Graham Bell, Thomas Edison, John D. Rockefeller, F. W. Woolworth and Theodore Roosevelt. He combined all the findings into a study course *The Law of Success*, and later in 1937 *Think and Grow Rich* was published which became a best seller is still in print today. Hill went on to become an advisor to presidents Woodrow Wilson and F. D. Roosevelt.

Hill explained that if we wanted to become rich we had to convince ourselves that we will acquire it. And, to achieve riches we had to drive ourselves into a white heat of emotion so that we are motivated to persist in our endeavours. Hill also emphasised the importance of focussed thinking which would lead to the physical realisation of our dreams. Hill strongly believed in the power of thoughts and dreams saying:

"You may as well know, also, that every great leader, from the dawn of civilisation, down to the present, was a dreamer. If you do not see great riches in your imagination, you will never see them in your bank balance. Never has there been so great an opportunity for practical dreamers as now exists."

According to Hill, there are six steps to becoming wealthy:
1. Fix in your mind the exact amount of money you desire.
2. Determine exactly what you intend to give in return for the money you desire. (There is no such reality as "something for nothing.")
3. Establish a definite date when you intend to possess the money you desire.
4. Create a definite plan for carrying out your desire, and begin at once, whether you are ready or not, to put this plan into action.
5. Write out a clear, concise statement of the amount of money you intend to acquire, name the time limit for its acquisition, state what you intend to give in return for the money, and describe clearly the plan through which you intend to accumulate it.
6. Read your written statement aloud, twice daily, once just before retiring at night, and once after arising in the morning. AS YOU READ – SEE AND FEEL AND BELIEVE YOURSELF ALREADY IN POSSESSION OF THE MONEY.

Napoleon Hill recognised the power of dreaming and said:

"Cherish your visions and your dreams as they are the children of your soul, the blueprints of your ultimate achievements."

116

RISK

Dreams may be free but acting on them is not without risk. How prepared are you to take risks? The history of humanity is closely linked to those who took risks. If people always stay with what they know and are comfortable there, they will not venture far. However, this can become boring and tiresome and most of us need some variety in our lives.

Staying at home is less dangerous than going out onto the streets but it is not without risks. More accidents happen in the home than anywhere else and if we stay at home too much we will become less healthy and become more prone to illness and disease. So, whether we realise it or not, whatever we do has some element of risk attached to it.

Women, in general, are less likely to take more challenging risks than men, and young men in particular are the biggest risk takers which explains why they have higher mortality rates. Yet, we need to take calculated risks. When the U.S. settlers travelled west to find new land and opportunities, they had dreams in their heads but they were also aware of the dangers which lay ahead of them. They had assessed the risks and rewards and concluded that it was worth setting out on this unknown journey.

Life is a journey into the future and there is no clear map which we can follow to guide us. The journey holds risks and rewards which we can tilt in our favour by thinking about many of the possible things which might happen and make plans about how to manage them if they do occur.

The level of risk which we are willing to take tends to decrease as we get older. This can be beneficial if it guides us to making better decisions about what to do. It can also be an obstacle to taking on new challenges and opportunities. Sometimes, we just have to make a leap of faith and trust that our preparations, knowledge and skills will help us succeed. As the wartime politician, Winston Churchill, described:

"The empires of the future are the empires of the mind."

IMAGINEERING

The word 'imagineering' a combination of 'imagination' and 'engineering' has become associated with the Walt Disney Company which is renowned for its ability to sprinkle pixie dust on a variety of projects and make them exciting. It is this ability to inspire and excite which has captivated people for many decades.

Imagineering was pioneered by the Alcoa corporation but it was Walt Disney who began as an artist and cartoonist who really captured the imaginations of people. His first animated film with a soundtrack was *Steamboat Willy* which involved Mickey Mouse and later *Snow White and the Seven Dwarves* received an Academy Award.

Since then Disney has expanded its operations and imagination blueprint to include theme parks, hotels and cruise ships at numerous locations across the world. Disney is particularly appealing to children with its exciting range of entertainment and also future oriented exhibitions.

The concept of imagineering continues to be used by a branch of Disney and the people who work there are called imagineers. These imagineers have contributed to many Disney innovations and have more than 100 patents for their technological and entertainment inventions. As Walt Disney said:

"If you can dream it, you can do it."

THE MEETING OF PREPARATION AND OPPORTUNITY

Have you ever decided to buy an item such as an automobile, clothing or electrical product etc.? Often before making the decision to buy you might have noticed how you see similar items in the street, magazines, or on television. This might be a coincidence, but in fact it is probably the result of the way in which you brain has adjusted to the instructions you have given it.

Let's suppose you are interested in a particular car model; you start thinking about its features, how many passengers it can carry; fuel consumption; colour etc. The more you think about the auto the more you focus your brain on it to the exclusion of any others in which you have no interest. Hundreds if not thousands of cars can pass you in the street yet you disregard them all because your attention is on that specific one. But as soon as your brain spots a car with all the features you are interested in it will draw your attention to it. This is like the cocktail party effect (see Chapter One) where you suddenly hear your name used despite all the noise around you.

This fine-tuning of your brain to only highlight certain signals is a very helpful skill which prevents your brain from becoming overloaded. It also helps you to identify things which are of interest to you and enables you to spot the needle in the haystack.

This ability to choose what we are looking for is an interesting one. For example, scan this page to identify where else the word 'cocktail' is located. Found it? Probably you will not have had to read every word on the page until you came to it, instead you directed your mind to find this word and it highlighted itself on the page and you disregarded all the other words in which you had no interest.

This is why mental preparation and rehearsal are so important to us. The more we practise and tune our minds into a particular area the more we become smarter at responding when the time comes to do it for real.

Also, if our minds are alert to something we are more likely to spot it which is why we increase the possibility of success. It is not necessarily luck which made us spot that bargain in the shop but the fact that we told our brains to be on the lookout for it. If we had not given this instruction we would have passed it by.

In other words we create our own luck by being mentally prepared so that when an opportunity occurs we are ready to swoop on it. As Louis Pasteur the French scientist who invented the process for removing TB from milk said:

"Fortune favours the prepared mind."

DID YOU SEE THE GORILLA?

Of course, the downside of this ability to focus on what we want to see means that we tend to disregard the rest. This is why people find information which supports their views and disregard information which is contrary to their preferred perspective. This is called confirmation bias and it can cause us problems. In one famous experiment Christopher Chabris and Daniel Simons asked people to watch a video and count the number of basketball passes a group of students made. At the same time, he arranged for a person in a gorilla costume to slowly walk through the group of players, beat its chest, and then exit the scene. When Simons asked the viewers, who had been counting the passes, if they had seen anything unusual, many hadn't and were stunned when they were shown a video tape of the events with the gorilla in the centre of the screen.

If we have not programmed our minds to look for something there is a strong possibility that we will not see it. For this reason it is often

120

valuable to keep an open mind so that we are able to spot more opportunities coming our way.

If we suspect we are looking at things only from one perspective we should intentionally consider contrary evidence to enable us to come to a balanced assessment. The next time you are looking for something in your home, office or refrigerator and you can't find it even though it is in clear view reconsider the situation. Did the image of the object in your mind accurately resemble the actual object? Sometimes just seeing the object from the wrong angle or incorrectly believing it is particular colour can make our brain reject it.

There are gorillas everywhere but if our concentration is on other things we will miss those hairy opportunities!

LUCKY DREAMS

CHANCE AND LUCK

Whether or not you have a lucky star it is important to understand the difference between chance and luck if you wish to give yourself the best opportunity of building your future. Although the two terms are often used interchangeably they do not really mean the same thing and this is why people become confused or waste valuable time and energy in chasing something which is unlikely to happen.

Firstly, let's begin by exploring what we mean by chance. Chance is the probability of something happening e.g. imagine there are a hundred people who each buy a ticket for a prize draw where the holder of the chosen ticket wins a high-tech television. If all the tickets are carefully shaken up in the hat the chance of winning is one in a hundred. If a person bought two tickets the chance would be one in fifty. Buying a ticket in the Euro-lottery and winning the jackpot has a one in 76million chance. There is a greater possibility of dying in a road accident!

If all you do to improve your future life is to buy a lottery ticket then you could be waiting a very long time. But someone has to win the jackpot which is why so many people give it a go. The ticket doesn't cost a lot and it allows people to let their dreams run wild and as we know this makes us feel better. Indeed, if you don't buy a ticket you will never win.

We all have an equal chance of winning the lottery if we buy a ticket. If we play sport and we train hard, eat the right food, and prepare carefully we will increase our chances of success. We have also seen that there are some people who are luckier than others because of the things which they do such as mixing with a wider range of people and persevering longer.

Lucky people don't win the lottery more than unlucky people because they both have an equal chance of winning. But in other areas of our lives, such as love and career success, attitude and preparation can make a significant improvement to our chances and make us luckier.

UNLUCKY – WRONG PLACE, WRONG TIME

Tsutomu Yamaguchi was a Japanese man sent by his employer Mitsubishi Heavy Industries to work in Hiroshima for three months. One day in August 1945 he saw an airplane drop two parachutes and very shortly afterwards there was a massive explosion and he instantly experienced the terror of a nuclear bomb. Fortunately he survived but the explosion had ruptured his eardrums, temporarily blinded him and given him burns on the left side of his body.

Yamaguchi sought safety overnight in a bomb-shelter and the next day he returned to his home in Nagasaki. Despite his injuries he reported for work two days later and informed his supervisor about the devastation he had witnessed. As he was doing so a second atomic bomb exploded just three kilometres away. Again he survived the destruction and surprisingly he was not alone, there were 165 double atomic-bomb survivors.

The chance of experiencing two nuclear bombs was very, very small but it happened. Of course, these people were also extremely unlucky to have been in the wrong place when two atomic bombs exploded but they might also be considered to have been very lucky to have survived. It is a matter of perspective.

Yamaguchi went on to live until he was 93 becoming a teacher, a campaigner against nuclear arms, and writing a book about his experiences. He warned about how military decisions regarding nuclear bombs could affect generations into the future. Are we listening?

MAKE YOUR OWN LUCK

Have you noticed how some people appear to be luckier than others in finding their dream partners and achieving their lifelong ambitions? They may not be exceptionally intelligent or talented but fortune smiles on them helping them to be in the right place at the right time.

This ability may be due to them being born under a lucky star but there is a strong possibility that they have created their own luck. The psychologist, Richard Wiseman, investigated luck and concluded that there were four main strategies used by lucky people and rarely used by unlucky people. Firstly, lucky people tend to be more extrovert and outgoing which results in them meeting more people. These interactions increase the possibility that they will encounter someone who can help them achieve their dreams. In addition, these people are more open and receptive to new opportunities and so became luckier.

Secondly, Wiseman suggests that people listen to their intuition. He described how we often use our unconscious to guide our decision making. For example, we may choose to buy a particular piece of clothing but not be fully able to explain why yet, later, people remark on how it really suits us. The same applies to financial and personal decisions and we should listen carefully to our inner thoughts because they may be picking up things which we are not consciously aware of. Is that investment a good choice? Is that person really reliable and honest?

The third finding by Wiseman was that: "Lucky people's dreams, ambitions and goals have an uncanny knack of coming true." These people have expectations about the future and they are generally positive e.g. they think they will have a good holiday and so they do. They think that something will work out and it does. Some of this luck is down to the self-fulfilling prophecy (which is described in Chapter 1) which describes how, if we expect something good, we will work hard and persist in making it happen.

The final observation by Wiseman was that unlucky people tell themselves they are unlucky and tend to dwell on their misfortune and do nothing to turn things around. Conversely, lucky people acknowledge that even when things go wrong, as they do for everyone, they adopt a positive perspective that it will all work out for the best in the long term. They also turn the bad luck into good luck and take practical steps to make sure that the same circumstances don't happen again in the future.

It seems that we can create our own luck and as Seneca, the Roman philosopher and statesman (4BC – 65AD) said:

"Luck is the meeting of preparation with opportunity."

THE MORE I PRACTISE THE LUCKIER I GET

The South African golfer, Gary Player, was once accused of being a lucky golfer and so he responded by saying: "You know what? The more I practise the luckier I get!" In other words, it was the fact that he spent so much time practising his shots that those golf balls which would have missed the hole in the past now came so close that they sometimes rolled in off the edge. His competitors thought he was just lucky but his secret was talent combined with hard work.

And it isn't just golf, we can improve our luck across most areas of our lives if we practise and persevere. We might not win every time but we will certainly increase our chances of success. And one of the best ways of being successful is to get as much practice as you possibly can.

Studies of professional sportspeople in the fields of football, soccer, ice-hockey etc have found that the majority were the older kids in their school year-groups. A few months difference in age can translate into a larger size, more knowledge and increased skills with the result that the older kids tend to perform better. The result means that they get picked more often for teams and, therefore, get more practise and experience and so become better and better relative to their younger classmates.

But we can all overcome this age disadvantage if we get that all important practice. It is said that we need 10,000 hours of practise to become successful and this enabled *The Beatles* pop group to be phenomenally successful. Before they became world famous they were invited to play in Hamburg, Germany and on their first trip they played for five hours or more a night for more than 100 nights. In following visits they also played a lot and it is estimated that by the time they hit the big-time in 1964 they had played live some 1,200 times. This is far more than most groups do these days and perhaps reflects the reason why their music endures to this day.

THE DREAM FACTORY

When you hear the word 'Hollywood' what images does it conjure up in your mind? Perhaps it is the glamorous movie stars standing on the red carpet at the Oscar ceremony while the paparazzi and television cameras transmit the images to millions around the world. Or maybe it is the movie studios where the films are created or perhaps it is the Hollywood walk of fame where the stars embedded in the sidewalk bring to mind Greta Garbo, Tom Cruise etc.

Hollywood is known as the *Dream Factory* because it has this remarkable ability to identify what appeals to us and create a dream world where almost anything is possible. We enter a darkened room and for approximately two hours are transported to other places, other times, other lives and we almost become those people experiencing their emotions as they fight their way to overcoming whatever challenges they face.

Hollywood has become a world leader in the production of films since D.

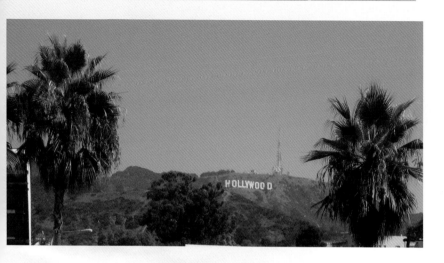

W. Griffith recorded the motion picture, *In Old California* in Hollywood in 1910. From this time it has attracted aspiring actors and many other people who dream of making it 'big'. The history and reputation of Hollywood was been built on its ability to visualize people's dreams.

WE ALL DREAM, BUT NOT EQUALLY

Most of us have had those late night conversations when all sorts of ideas and plans come tumbling out. Many of them appear achievable when we have support around us and we are insulated from the reality of the outside world. All we have to do is begin to follow the dream the next day.

However, when dawn arrives it often seems that the bright sunbeams penetrate the darkest corners of our dreams and reveal reasons why they might not be possible. All our optimism and commitment from just a few hours previously seems to drain away as we resume everyday tasks.

Perhaps it is the reality of the daytime which makes us explore more critically the dreams which we had the night before. Yet, if we interrogate them and share them with a variety of people we are more likely to get a wider range of insights and evaluations. Some will like our dreams, some will be politely neutral and others will pour cold water on them.

We should not necessarily be disheartened by negative comments. If they are delivered properly they should be directed at the ideas and not the dreamer. Instead, we should use all the feedback and weigh the positives and negatives coming to a balanced conclusion about whether or not to follow this particular dream.

It is important not to lose heart; if it was good last night then there must have been something intrinsically powerful and motivating. We just have to summon up the courage and motivation to deliver it and, as we will see below, there are people who can do just that. As Lawrence of Arabia (1888-1935) observed:

> *"All men dream: but not equally. Those who dream by night in the dusty recesses of their minds wake in the day to find that it was vanity: but the dreamers of the day are dangerous men, for they may act their dreams with open eyes, to make it possible."*

THE EDEN PROJECT

Tim Smit has one of those unusual names that reads the same backwards as well as forwards. More importantly, he is one of those dreamers who not only has a big idea but also can convert it into reality. One of his first major ideas was to take a run-down house and over-grown gardens in Cornwall, at the south-west tip of England, and restore it into a major visitor attraction for people who love gardens and gardening. He believed in the idea that if you build it people will come and visit.

Smit and a close group of colleagues pooled their enthusiasm, knowledge and skills to resurrect the beautiful Victorian garden which fell into decay when the gardeners enlisted into the army and went off to fight in the Great War and never returned. Smit wrote that many people talk about their dreams of what they would like to do but often never get round to doing anything and thus despair of ever achieving them. He wrote:

"The pipe dream comes alive for a happy hour or two but does it fade by morning, leaving that growing sense of self-hatred as you realise you haven't got what it takes to do the interesting or brave thing?"

The restoration of the Lost Gardens of Heligan taught Smit and his team about the importance of hard work and commitment to the task of achieving their dream. They realised that everyone has dreams but few develop the ability of turning them into reality. Smit said:

"No one has a monopoly on dreams, but only a rare few discover the alchemist's art of making them real."

He said that the secret of making dreams materialise was a determined commitment and single-mindedness to succeed. It also required a convincing idea and the powerful ability to inspire and transfer that conviction to other people.

Some people stop when they achieve their dream but Smit and his colleagues were inspired by their success to dream even bigger dreams. Late one night, while sharing a glass or two of the hard-stuff, they developed the concept of five large connected greenhouses or poly-tunnels each of which represented a climatic zone containing plants from that geographical area.

Slowly, but surely, through the power of persuasion and hard work they convinced government and other funding sources and so raised £80 million ($120m) to build their project in an old clay pit and reclaim the land. The greenhouses, or biomes, are the largest conservatory in the world at 240m long, 110m wide and 50m high.

The project became known as the Eden Project and since it opened some 10 million people have visited the site and enjoyed this extraordinary venture. It is an educational charity which has helped rejuvenate the local economy and inspired countless people to think environmentally. Numerous events, concerts and educational courses have been held which have encouraged visitors to dream their own dreams of improving the environment for themselves and the communities they work with.

Ode

We are the music makers,
And we are the dreamer of dreams,
Wandering by lone sea-breakers,
And sitting by desolate streams;
World-losers and world-forsakers,
On whom the pale moon gleams:
Yet we are the movers and shakers
Of the world for ever, it seems.

With wonderful deathless ditties,
We build up the world's great cities,
And out of a fabulous story
We fashion an empire's glory:
One man with a dream, at pleasure,
Shall go forth and conquer a crown;
And three with a new song's measure
Can trample an empire down.

We, in the ages lying
In the buried past of earth,
Built Nineveh with our sighing,
And Babel itself with our mirth;
And o'erthrew them with prophesying
To the old of the new world's worth;
For each age is a dream that is dying,
Or one that is coming to birth.

A breath of our inspiration,
Is the life of each generation.

A wondrous thing of our dreaming,
Unearthly, impossible seeming-
The soldier, the king, and the peasant
Are working together in one,
Till our dream shall become their present,
And their work in the world be done.

They had no vision amazing
Of the goodly house they are raising.
They had no divine foreshowing
Of the land to which they are going:
But on one man's soul it hath broke,
A light that doth not depart
And his look, or a word he hath spoken,
Wrought flame in another man's heart.

And therefore today is thrilling,
With a past day's late fulfilling.
And the multitudes are enlisted
In the faith that their fathers resisted,
And, scorning the dream of tomorrow,
Are bringing to pass, as they may,
In the world, for it's joy or it's sorrow,
The dream that was scorned yesterday.

But we, with our dreaming and singing,
Ceaseless and sorrowless we!
The glory about us clinging
Of the glorious futures we see,
Our souls with high music ringing;

O men! It must ever be
That we dwell, in our dreaming and singing,
A little apart from ye.

For we are afar with the dawning
And the suns that are not yet high,
And out of the infinite morning
Intrepid you hear us cry –
How, spite of your human scorning,
Once more God's future draws nigh,
And already goes forth the warning
That ye of the past must die.

Great hail! we cry to the corners
From the dazzling unknown shore;
Bring us hither your sun and your summers,
And renew our world as of yore;
You shall teach us your song's new numbers,
And things that we dreamt not before;
Yea, in spite of a dreamer who slumbers,
And a singer who sings no more.

ARTHUR O'SHAUGHNESSY (1844-1881) BRITISH POET

DREAM SUMMARIES

- Achieving our dreams requires hard work and perseverance.

- The world is complex and many things can cause our dreams to disappear.

- The butterfly effect illustrates the possibilities of even small changes.

- Martin Luther King Jr had a dream which inspired millions of people.

- Anticipation will help us achieve our dreams and even our wealth.

- The more we practise the luckier we get.

- Luck is the meeting of preparation and opportunity.

- We all dream and everything begins with a dream.

- Achieving a dream requires courage and perseverance.

6
CREATIVE DREAMS

"Imagination is more important than knowledge for while knowledge defines all we currently know and understand, imagination points to all we might yet discover and create."
ALBERT EINSTEIN (1879-1955) THEORETICAL PHYSICIST

INTRODUCTION

Our sleep dreams at night are very important to us and without them we would not be able to function properly the following day. They may also be messages from our unconscious which need interpretation as well as being a source of creativity. Of no less importance are our dreams during the day when we naturally generate ideas either consciously or subconsciously.

Creativity requires the ability to dream and the better a person's skills of dreaming the greater the chances of successful creativity whether it is music, art, drama, architecture, design, sport etc.

The inspiration for our dreams sometimes comes internally and it may not always be clear how they originated. Dreams can also be inspired externally e.g. from the natural environment which inspired many poets, or from charismatic people who demonstrated what ordinary people could achieve. This chapter examines these productive areas and draws encouragement from a number of creative and sporting people.

SLEEP DREAMS

DREAMING IN OUR SLEEP

In the past, the ancients considered dreams in our sleep as messages from the gods or as predictions of the future. Yet sleep dreams are notoriously difficult to understand and interpret, and also they are very easy to forget as soon as we become fully awake. This confusion was described by the Ancient Greek philosopher Homer who said that there were true dreams and false dreams. In *The Odyssey* he wrote:

"There are two gates through which these insubstantial visions reach us,

one is of horn, and the other of ivory. Those that come through the ivory gate cheat us with empty promises that never see fulfilment; while those that issue from the gate of burnished horn inform the dreamer what will really happen."

When we are asleep our dreams tend to be more unusual and exotic than those we have during our waking hours and this mysterious dream world is slowly being revealed in sleep laboratories and other research centres. One very interesting area of study involves lucid dreaming where a sleeping person is also aware that they are dreaming. This occasionally happens to many people but there are some who have greater control of their dreaming. In one experiment, these people clenched their fist in their dreams and a brain scanner was able to detect this imaginary movement. The area of the brain which was activated was exactly the same as if it were being done in real life.

It appears that our dreams are very real to us and it is possible that sometimes they may reveal something about our innermost thoughts and desires. The founder of psychoanalysis, Sigmund Freud, wrote a book, *The Interpretation of Dreams*, which provided guidance on the meaning of dreams and many people analyse, interpret and use them to guide and shape what they will do. But how much attention should we give to our dreams and how do we interpret which are 'good' dreams and which are 'bad' dreams? In fact, there is no clear answer to these questions and we should think carefully before we decide to follow the guidance of our sleep dreams. Whether or not we act on our dreams, may they all be 'Sweet Dreams.'

SLEEP DREAMS ARE GOOD FOR YOU

People who lack sleep are often forgetful, grumpy, and groggy, and are unable to function very well. It seems that we need sleep to help our brains operate more effectively and so improve our language, memory and flexibility of thought. No one quite understands how it helps us but it is very clear that we cannot operate well if we do not get a good night's sleep.

How much sleep we need depends on the individual. Some people function well with just a few hours e.g. Florence Nightingale; others need eight, ten or even more hours, and children and young people sleep for longer periods than adults and older people. If we are sleepy during the daytime it is probably a sign that we need to increase the amount of sleep which we get.

There are periods of sleep which are called REM-sleep during which there is rapid eye movement hence the name. It is during this REM sleep that we experience most of our dreams and if these dreams are interrupted we tend to function much more poorly the next day.

When we go to sleep, we may sometimes notice that we 'fall off a log' or give a shake just as we drift off into sleep. This is a sign that our body is being disconnected from actively following our mental thoughts, otherwise we might spend our nights actually running down the street in our pyjamas or undertaking all sorts of bizarre actions.

There are some people who are able to recognise when they are dreaming and control their dreams and this is called lucid dreaming. One of the foremost researchers into the subject suggested that, "We are dreaming all the time but when we are awake we are influenced by our senses."

It is sometimes hard to make decisions when there is too much detail or our minds are tired. Therefore, it is often a good idea to sleep on a problem because it would appear that during the night our thoughts are organized more effectively. The next morning we can see the problem more clearly and are able to identify a solution. It would appear that night dreams can sometimes help us achieve our daydreams.

DREAMS INCUBATION

Sleeping on a problem or allowing our minds to incubate a dream is a practice used by many people who realise that time is needed to refine the concept so that it gets closer to perfection. The children's author, Michael Murpurgo, not only fires up the imagination of children with his books, one of his books *War Horse* was turned into a highly successful stage show which was adored by adults and theatre critics, and subsequently was made into a film. In the stage show three 'operatives' manipulate a wire-frame horse and these people are clearly visible to the audience. Yet, in spite of this apparent intrusion, the audience's imaginations soon lose awareness of the operators controlling the horse and become totally immersed in the story.

Morpurgo recognises the importance of letting his ideas germinate and encourages his imagination to work which often takes time:

"I spend months, sometimes years, doing what I call dreamtime, weaving it together inside my head. But when I actually feel that the egg of my story is ready to hatch, then I can write it in three months. Then I know the landscape and the people well and from the inside, but I don't necessarily know where the story is taking us."

WE ARE ALL CREATIVE

CREATIVITY AND INVENTION

Creativity is often associated with extraordinarily talented individuals such as Mozart, Leonardo da Vinci, Thomas Edison etc. At another level there is also a perspective that only certain people are creative such as artists, jazz musicians, architects etc. but the reality is that we are all creative. For example, when we construct a sentence the likelihood of someone stringing that specific group of words together is almost impossible. Similarly, events which happen to us during the day are unique and therefore our responses to them will also be unique and therefore creative.

Once we realise that we are creative we can unleash these talents more widely if we have confidence and belief in ourselves. We can take up new creative hobbies such as painting, designing, writing and so on, the only thing holding us back is our reluctance to explore our dreams of what we might do and become.

Letting our minds wander and daydream is sometimes a very productive way of finding a solution to a problem which we are wrestling with. Our minds just suddenly throw out the answer without us even thinking directly about it and this can happen when we are doing housework, walking and even bathing. The ancient Greek scholar Archimedes once stepped into a bath and noticed the water rising and cried "Eureka" meaning, "I have found it." He had suddenly understood that the displacement of water provided the solution to measuring the volume of irregularly shaped objects.

It is clear that inspiration can be found in many situations, even bathing, and this depends on having an open and receptive mind to new ideas and seeing things in different ways. As George Bernard Shaw, the Irish playwright, explained:

"You see things; and you say, 'Why?' But I dream things that never were; and I say, 'Why not?' "

We are all creative and we all dream which is a delicious combination. Together they can be used to make remarkable futures for ourselves. As Peter Drucker, the management writer said:

"The best way to predict your future is to create it."

CREATIVE ART

Creative people often speak of a tension or pressure inside them which has to be expressed in some form or another. This can be particularly common with artists who feel unable to settle until they release this dam holding back their ideas.

Often, an idea or concept comes into a person's mind but it can be rapidly lost and drowned out by the noise of other incoming thoughts. Perhaps it was a particular line of reasoning or combination of circumstances which acted together to create that insight for just a split second. However, that wonderful spontaneous amalgamation of thoughts is rapidly lost. For artists this can be particularly troublesome because they may have a flash of inspiration and if they don't capture it immediately they know that it will vanish. This explains why, when an image takes hold, they have to drop everything they are currently doing and focus intensively on materialising their creative ideas.

A frequent time to come up with good ideas is when the mind is unwinding just before we go to sleep. However, if we wait until the morning the idea is often lost and so it is really advisable to have a note pad by the bed to jot down the idea. It can then be returned to in the morning although there are some people who cannot rest once they have an idea and the only solution is to get up and begin the creative downloading process.

The poet Samuel Taylor Coleridge dreamed a poem in his sleep and when he awoke he immediately began writing so that he would not forget and he titled it *Kubla Khan: or A Vision in a Dream*. Although Coleridge believed he had remembered all the words from his dream and had begun to write them all down, he was interrupted by a visitor and then lost the end of the poem which remained uncompleted.

Throughout this book we have explained that first we need to dream about something before we can bring it about. This is a form of mental creativity in which we can explore things from many, many perspectives. Pablo Picasso, the Spanish artist held the view that:

"Everything you can imagine is real."

And Vincent Van Gogh, the Dutch impressionist painter vividly used his imagination to inform his work. Mental visualisation was fundamentally important to him and he explained the process which he used: "I dream of painting then I paint the dream."

DREAM IT FIRST

To achieve excellence it is first necessary to know what is needed. We have to visualize what we want to achieve before we can set out on the road to achieving our dreams. Whatever walk of life a person follows they can only achieve what they wish if they imagine it.

The English rugby player, Jonny Wilkinson, had a remarkable career becoming the record points scorer in international rugby. In the final of the Rugby World Cup between Australia and England both teams were tied on 14-14 with only seconds remaining of extra-time. Then, with more than 80,000 spectators and many millions watching on TV, he kept his composure and succeeded in kicking the ball between the posts to secure the World Championship.

Wilkinson's ability to consistently and successfully kick the ball didn't just happen overnight. It took hours of practice every day over many years to develop this skill. In particular, he was famous for his ability to concentrate and follow a careful routine involving gripping his hands together and looking to where he wanted to kick the ball. This visualisation was a key component to his success and he later said:

"I cannot overestimate how much controlling the mind is crucial to my life as a goal-kicker in rugby union. You have to be able to see perfection before you can achieve it."

THOUGHT EXPERIMENTS

When we imagine doing something we are mentally testing out whether or not it might be a good course of physical action in the future. We might try out several imaginative strategies before deciding on which is the best way of doing something and then we can mentally rehearse again and again until we get it right. We call this a thought experiment.

Thought experiments are not new, they have been used by many scientists throughout history to explore areas without actually doing them. And, even actual scientific experiments all begin in the minds of the scientists before they conduct them for real. Scientists conduct thought experiments for a number of reasons: they might not have the money or resources to do it for real; it might be too dangerous to carry out; and it might be currently impossible because they have not yet been invented.

Two of the most famous scientists the world has ever known have used thought experiments. Isaac Newton, who is credited with discovering gravity, imagined what might happen if he fired a cannon ball further and further until it fell over the horizon. He then imagined that the cannon ball continued falling but was held by the earth's gravitational field so that it kept moving around the earth like a satellite does today. Newton's thought experiments have paved the way for our modern communications technologies.

Albert Einstein is another scientist who has used thought experiments to advance human knowledge. When he was sixteen he imagined riding a beam of light which led to his famous theory of relativity $E = MC^2$. Fortunately, we do not need the enormous intelligence of Einstein to imagine, instead, we can just direct our minds to imagine whatever we like, possible or impossible. Just as Einstein imagined riding a light beam we can soar through the air like a bird, sit on clouds, and transport ourselves to our own tropical island.

"Thinking is an experimental dealing with small quantities of energy, just as a general moves miniature figures over a map before setting his troops in action."
SIGMUND FREUD (1856 – 1939) FOUNDER OF PSYCHOANALYSIS

DREAM SCULPTURE

Many communities around the world have found their lives turned upside-down by economic changes which have destroyed their local industries. This situation happened to a coalmining community in Saint Helens, England, where generations of families had been involved in the dangerous task of mining coal. When the colliery closed it left behind unemployment and a bleak landscape covered with spoil heaps and old buildings.

Gradually, urban renewal and nature turned the site into a green forested area again and made it more attractive to visitors. However, the community wanted to mark their history, create a focal point for their identity, and encourage regeneration and new jobs for themselves and their children. Slowly an idea emerged for a piece of artwork and when Channel 4 TV and Arts Council England ran a competition to encourage ordinary people to engage with art a community group decided to apply. The group, which included former miners, were surprised and delighted when their application was one of seven chosen from more than 1,400 applications.

Thus began the challenge of identifying an artist and a piece of art which would represent the area which lies midway between Liverpool and Manchester. The group settled on the Spanish artist Jaume Plensa and his first proposal was *The Miner's Soul* – a light on a plinth symbolising a miner's lamp. Unlike many inexperienced people who might follow the expert's decision, the group decided that this wasn't what they wanted. Instead, they explained that this looked backwards and they wanted something more forward looking and inspirational.

Plensa then shared with the group his original idea for the site which he thought would not be liked because it was too daring and conceptual. On seeing a model, the group were delighted and unanimously endorsed the construction of the sculpture – *Dream*.

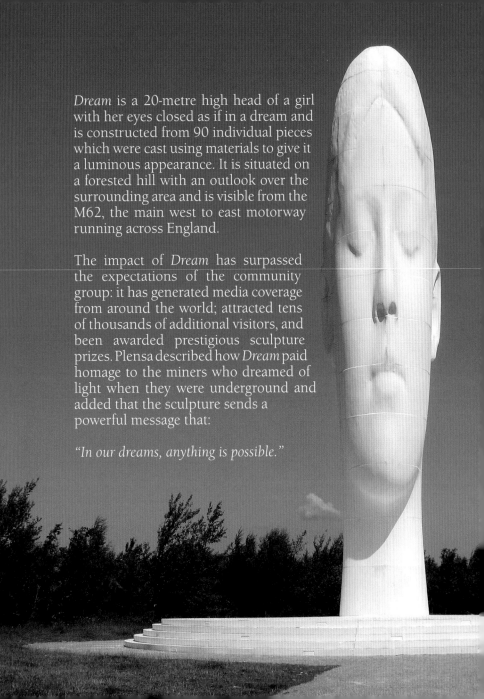

Dream is a 20-metre high head of a girl with her eyes closed as if in a dream and is constructed from 90 individual pieces which were cast using materials to give it a luminous appearance. It is situated on a forested hill with an outlook over the surrounding area and is visible from the M62, the main west to east motorway running across England.

The impact of *Dream* has surpassed the expectations of the community group: it has generated media coverage from around the world; attracted tens of thousands of additional visitors, and been awarded prestigious sculpture prizes. Plensa described how *Dream* paid homage to the miners who dreamed of light when they were underground and added that the sculpture sends a powerful message that:

"In our dreams, anything is possible."

CREATIVE INSPIRATION

SOURCES OF INSPIRATION

Inspiration comes from two main sources, either from deep within us or from some person or something outside us. Yet, there is a problem with inspiration in that it is very hard to capture or to bottle so that it can be used whenever there is a need.

The memories and jottings of many great creative writers and artists are littered with remarks about how they sometimes found their occupation hard going. They sat in front of empty pages or canvasses and wondered how they were going to fill the blank space. Inspiration did not appear on demand and they were left without the motivation to begin their work. So, to get around these mental blocks, they had to force themselves to work through the barren periods until they achieved their objectives. In fact, many creative people recognise that their output is sometimes 1% inspiration and 99% perspiration.

But inspiration, however small, is an essential ingredient for creative people. This book has described several times how we tend not to see things which surround us all the time. This is beneficial because paying close attention to everything about us would fill our heads with too much detail and this would overload our processing capacity. Instead, our brains scan the environment and if there is no major change it just keeps us on automatic pilot.

But there is a snag. If we are surrounded by the same things everyday eventually they blur into the background and disappear from our consciousness. Therefore, we need to stimulate ourselves by exploring new situations, places, ideas, and people. And, the more we expose ourselves to new things the greater the potential will be that we are stimulated and possibly inspired to integrate them into our activities.

Our interactions with other people have the potential to inspire and influence the way they think and behave. Those who regularly interact with children and young people, such as teachers, have a particular responsibility to model actions because these are often copied. Young children in particular tend to copy the behaviour of each other and it becomes contagious and spreads rapidly.

In fact, we all tend to observe other people, reflect on it and think to ourselves: "We can do that." This is why some organisations invite people to speak and inspire their staff perhaps with stories about overcoming adversity or developing a new product or business. This is also why print advertisements and TV commercials present famous people using their products.

Our imaginative ability varies, and often it takes a little push to get it going. And, this push generally comes from seeing other people achieve things which inspires us to give it a go. As Mark Twain said:

"Really great people make you feel that you, too, can become great."

150

TREAD CAREFULLY FOR YOU TREAD ON MY DREAMS

We hold our dreams close to our hearts and are very protective of them since we have conceived them, nurtured them and want to deliver them as fully formed concepts. And, because they are ever present in our minds and close to the surface it is natural that we will speak about them.

But, other people can fail to understand or see the benefits of a new idea since they haven't spent the same amount of time and energy exploring all the possibilities. Revolutionary ideas are, by definition, not conventional and the majority of people are happier with slow change rather than revolutionary change. If something is new it can be very hard for them to comprehend and tune into a completely different idea. Therefore, they should be given time and space to fully absorb an idea and we should not be upset if their views do not correspond with our own.

"But I, being poor, have only my dreams; I have spread my dreams beneath your feet. Tread softly because you tread on my dreams."
W.B. YEATS (1865 – 1935) IRISH POET AND PLAYWRIGHT

Indeed, seeking out alternative views can be a sensible and practical way of testing how durable a dream is. Different insights may help to advance the dream by providing practical suggestions; however, if people continue to dismiss our dreams then perhaps it is wise to really try and see things from their perspective. If people can't get their heads around our vision they are less likely to give us the support which we may need. And, if we need their support, we will need to think of ways in which we can communicate our vision more clearly and successfully. If we don't, and we need these people, then we will fail to realise the dream.

On the other hand failure of people to understand our dream can be an advantage. If no one has thought of it before then there may be an opportunity in the marketplace for a new product or service. There will be no competition and we will get a head start if we don't communicate the innovative idea too widely. The inventor of the wind-up radio and flashlight, Trevor Bayliss, said:

"May all your dreams be patentable."

ARCHITECTURAL DREAMS

Friedrich Froebel was a German educational pioneer who developed the concept of the kindergarten where children could be nurtured and encouraged so that they learned successfully and grew into mature adults each with their own personalities and qualities. Rather than being systematically taught which could sometimes become boring and demotivate the children he encouraged discovery learning. This involved providing them with what became known as Froebel Gifts and which included wooden geometric blocks, balls, string and sticks.

The children were then mainly left to play as they wanted and create shapes and build structures etc. Playing with these 'gifts' allowed the children to develop their understanding of shapes, spatial awareness, construction, touch etc. and they were allowed to progress at their own speed.

At the 1876 Centennial Exposition held in Philadelphia there was a Friedrich Froebel Kindergarten exhibit which displayed the 'gifts'. Some of the wooden blocks were bought by Anna Wright who used them to encourage and educate her son. Little did she know at the time that she was planting the seeds and encouraging the imagination of one of the USA's greatest architects, Frank Lloyd Wright. The strong designs of his buildings clearly reflect his early experiences with the

Froebel gifts and in his writings he said:

> *"The maple-wood blocks... all are in my fingers to this day."*
> *"The smooth shapely maple blocks with which to build, the sense of which never afterward leaves the fingers: so form became feeling."*

DREAM SUMMARIES

- Sleep dreams are beneficial to our health and well-being.

- It is sometimes best to allow our dreams to incubate and develop slowly so that they mature into fully formed and applicable ideas.

- If you want to create your future you must first dream it.

- We need to develop our powers of dreaming which will then help us to be more creative and inventive.

- Many scientists use thought experiments to help them conduct research in an inexpensive way.

- We can inspire ourselves and be inspired by other people and things around us.

7
YOUR LIFE YOUR FUTURE

"I like the dreams of the future better than the history of the past."
THOMAS JEFFERSON (1743 – 1826) FOUNDING FATHER AND US PRESIDENT

"The vast possibilities of our great future will become realities only if we make ourselves responsible for that future."
GIFFORD PINCHOT (1865 – 1946) FIRST CHIEF OF US FOREST SERVICE

INTRODUCTION

In the movie, *The Man Who Knew Too Much*, Doris Day sang the well-known song *Que Sera Sera*. Translated from the French this means, what will be, will be; and it highlights the fact that it is very difficult to look into the future. It is hard to predict the future and the further into the future we peer the more challenging this becomes. Weather forecasters face a similar problem and although they are reasonably accurate for a few days ahead after that their accuracy becomes close to guesswork. But there is a difference; we might not be able to change the weather but we can change our behaviour according to the prevailing conditions. Changeable winds can influence a sailboat; however, if we have a clear understanding of the direction of our dreams we can adjust the sails and the rudder and still arrive at our destination.

In this chapter we will explore how we can use mental time travel to guide us on our journey through life. We cannot predict everything which we might encounter but if we can see a few steps ahead this will enable us to set out on the journey and deal with the challenges which we will inevitably face. There will probably be some broken dreams along the way but if we have a store of dreams we can always make alternative plans and build a new future.

LIFE PLANNING

PLAN YOUR LIFE

We spend a great deal of time looking forward to vacations and when they arrive we want to relax and enjoy our time as much as possible. To do this we carefully find out about our destination, accommodation, food etc. and then arrange things so that they come as close to perfection as possible thereby giving us wonderful memories which can keep us going through the winter months.

Our vacation time is valuable and that is why we want to get the most from it. And, you would think, this attitude would also apply to achieving the most from our lives, but many people spend more time planning their vacations than on planning their lives. There are many reasons why this is so. Perhaps we are too familiar with our everyday lives. Perhaps we think that there is plenty of time to cram everything in. Perhaps we think we can do that hard thinking another day when we have more time. Perhaps we are too satisfied with how things are than to plan for the future. There are so many excuses but few of them stand up to scrutiny for very long.

We cannot expect anyone else to plan our lives for us. It is our responsibility for making space in our lives to consider what we would really like and then to prioritise these dreams and then to set out a route map to achieving them. We might also encourage children to think about what they want to do and give them plenty of encouragement. Working away at dreary homework is not motivating for most children but if they can see a bright future for themselves they will stick to the task and be successful.

If we value ourselves and what we can contribute to those around us we should plan what we want to achieve. The old saying: 'People don't plan to fail, they fail to plan' is very accurate. The more thought which we invest in planning where we want to go in our lives the greater the chance we will achieve what we want for ourselves and our families.

"Le futur n'est pas ce qui vient vers nous, mais ce vers quoi nous allons."
"The future is not what is coming at us, but what we are headed for."
JEAN-MARIE GUYAU (1854 – 1888) FRENCH PHILOSOPHER AND POET

MENTAL TIME TRAVEL

"We all have our time machines. Some take us back, they're called memories. Some take us forward, they're called dreams."
JEREMY IRONS, ACTOR

In 1895 the author H.G. Wells wrote *The Time Machine* and captured people's imaginations with a tale of how a time machine had been invented which enabled a traveller to go forwards and backwards in time. Wells wrote:

"We all saw the lever turn. I am absolutely certain there was no trickery. There was a breath of wind, and the lamp flame jumped. One of the candles on the mantel was blown out, and the little machine suddenly swung round, became indistinct, was seen as a ghost for a second perhaps, as an eddy of faintly glittering brass and ivory; and it was gone — vanished!"

Since the book was written there has been much interest in time travel and constructing machines which might transport us in time but none of it has materialised. Despite this many people lose sight of the fact that we all possess a time machine – it is our brain, and our memories take us backwards to revisit past events; or can take us forwards to dream and explore things which might happen in the future.

This fantastic ability of our brains for mental time travel was described by the Canadian psychologist Endel Tulving who explained that this capability enhanced our skills for living. For example, there are times when events happen so quickly that we cannot fully make sense of what is going on. Afterwards we can use our memories to revisit them, understand them and learn from them. Similarly, we can mentally time travel into the future and explore possible situations thus learning from them and helping us make appropriate choices when we eventually face them in real life.

"It's a poor sort of memory that only works backwards,"
the Queen remarked.
Lewis Carroll (1832 – 1898) Through the Looking Glass

The First Step

It is hugely difficult if not impossible to predict the future and there is no crystal ball to help us see through the fog ahead. For some people, this uncertainty can be frightening and for others exhilarating. But, as the Chinese proverb advises, all journeys begin with a first step, and if we don't take that first step we will stay where we are and fail to advance.

Of course, the steps which we can take are not all the same. Some are relatively tiny ones which allow us to check things out without committing everything. Some steps even allow us to return back to where we were because we did not like what we were experiencing. It is like putting our toes into the water to check the temperature is OK. However, some steps are almost irreversible such as when we hand in our job resignation letter, or sign a contract for a car or a house.

Before we take those momentous steps we should use our imaginations to explore what it will be like to be in that new situation. What will the circumstances be like, what is the other person / people going to be like? The more we can mentally explore the better we will get a feeling for what it will be like.

Thinking about what it will be like when we make those first steps will give us the opportunity to rehearse how we will respond rather than being tongue-tied or perhaps hiding away until we can make sense of our new environment.

Also, we sometimes need courage to take those first steps and, no matter how hard we try to visualize what it will be like, there will be things which we have not thought about or things which will only happen if we take those steps.

"Just take the first step in faith. You don't have to see the whole staircase. Just take the first step."
MARTIN LUTHER KING JR. (1929 – 1968) CLERGYMAN AND CIVIL RIGHTS LEADER

OUTWARD BOUND

The term 'outward bound' is a nautical expression which describes a ship leaving a harbour. When it stays in the harbour it is safe but that is not the purpose of a ship; it needs to embark on a journey and face challenges and possible dangers in order to reach its destination.

> *"A ship in harbour is safe, but that is not what ships are built for."*
> JOHN AUGUSTUS SHEDD

We too will remain relatively safe if we stay comfortable where we are but we will eventually become supremely bored, lack stimulation and probably lose any initiative which we once had. Just look around you at people who once were highly energetic and involved in everything and who now seem to have the lost their spark. They have probably lost that interest in new things, people, ideas and experiences. Of course, not much harm may befall us if we stay safe, but that was not what we were designed to do. We were meant to go out and explore and discover new opportunities.

During the Second World War it was found that when ships belonging to the Atlantic convoys were torpedoed it was the older sailors who tended to survive rather than the younger fitter ones. The reason for this was that the older sailors had much more life experience and were therefore better able to handle adversity, whereas the younger more inexperienced sailors tended to succumb more easily.

Lawrence Holt, a director of the Blue Funnel shipping line, and Kurt Hahn the Headmaster of Gordonstoun School established an Outward Bound school in 1941 to train young seamen to handle difficult situations by using the outdoors. Since then the Outward Bound charity has been established in many countries and has enabled many young people to develop more resilient life skills through adventuring outside their safe harbours.

SET SAIL

As life proceeds, it is possible that some of our main regrets will not be about the things which we have done, but will be more focussed on what we haven't done e.g. what held us back from speaking to that person who might have changed our lives for ever? Why didn't we save for that rainy day? Why didn't we give more support to someone who needed it?

Do you look back on elements of your life and wish that you had done something differently? You are not alone in reminiscing about what might have been and how things might have turned out differently. Yet, as long as we don't bury ourselves in the past this is probably quite a helpful thing as it teaches us what went wrong and how we might act differently in the future and thus prevent the same mistakes happening again. Essentially, reflecting on the past is a constructive learning tool which helps us to develop strategies for handling situations in the future.

So, in order to minimise future regrets we should carefully assess opportunities and then set sail to explore them. As Mark Twain said:

"Twenty years from now you will be more disappointed by the things you didn't do than by the ones you did do. So throw off the bowlines. Sail away from the safe harbor. Catch the trade winds in your sails. Explore. Dream. Discover."

HEADLIGHTS

One of the things which sometimes holds people back from achieving their dreams is the fear that they cannot clearly see where they are going. They may know that they want to be happy, successful, rich, famous etc. but they are afraid because the route is undefined.

One way to overcome this hurdle is to imagine a long automobile journey travelling only at night. Because of the darkness we are only able to see as far as the headlights illuminate the road in front of us. However, this should not stop us from making the journey, we only have to see a reasonable distance along the road to drive safely and reach our destination successfully. And, as we proceed the headlights progressively reveal the shape and contours of the road ahead and so we can carry out our expedition across the length and breadth of the country.

We can also use this image of headlights to support us in another way. If we have headlights which are brighter and cast their light further they enable us to see further and so identify possible opportunities or even dangers on the journey. To see further into the future we need to do our homework. This means educating ourselves; researching, and learning as much as we can about what we want to achieve. The more we know the more we can make the best decisions because we have identified the opportunities and roadblocks along the route.

Also, if our research and imaginations are more advanced than other people we will understand more thus helping us to make more informed decisions. This can provide a distinct advantage when making choices about investments, purchases, and life decisions.

PICKING YOURSELF UP

VICTIM OF HISTORY OR MASTER OF MY FATE

Invictus
Out of the night that covers me,
Black as the pit from pole to pole,
I thank whatever gods may be,
For my unconquerable soul.

In the fell clutch of circumstance
I have not winced nor cried aloud.
Under the bludgeonings of chance
My head is bloody, but unbowed.

Beyond this place of wrath and tears
Looms but the horror of the shade,
And yet the menace of the years
Finds, and shall find, me unafraid.

It matters not how strait the gate,
How charged with punishments the scroll.
I am the master of my fate:
The captain of my soul.

WILLIAM ERNEST HENLEY (1849 – 1903) ENGLISH POET

It is one of the most profound questions which humans ask themselves: "Is my destiny in my own hands or does fate decide?" This is an exceptionally deep spiritual and philosophical question and one that has never been fully answered nor agreed. Yet, whatever the answer might be, we should not just allow ourselves to accept everything which comes at us and take no responsibility for our destiny. Around the world there are proverbs which indicate the balance between the forces of man and divine power. Some people say, "Trust in God, but lock your car", and elsewhere, they say, "Trust in Allah, but tie your camel."

The Victorian poet William Ernest Henley wrote the inspirational poem – *Invictus*, meaning undefeated or unconquered, which concludes with these lines:

> *"I am the master of my fate:*
> *I am the captain of my soul."*

In some ways the poem is quite dark and reflects the stoicism, the patience in adversity, which is sometimes necessary to help us through difficult times. In relates to the fact that when Henley was young, he caught tuberculosis which resulted in one of his lower legs being amputated. Henley realised that he could wallow in this misfortune and let it hinder the rest of his life or he could take control of his future. He chose the latter and his poem has encouraged countless people to press on when times were difficult and life seemed to have little meaning.

The poem is so powerful and inspiring that Nelson Mandela used it to raise his spirits during the 27 years he spent imprisoned on Robben Island. Later, when he was released and had become president of South Africa he attended a rugby match and saw that the black spectators were cheering the opposition because they felt that the South African team represented apartheid. Mandela met with François Pienaar, the captain of the South African rugby team, and expressed his concern that the forthcoming Rugby World Cup was an opportunity for the whole country to unite behind the team. He shared Henley's *Invictus* poem with Pienaar and, subsequently, with the support of the nation, the team went on to win the cup. The exploits were recreated in a film called *Invictus* and, at the end, as the people of different backgrounds were celebrating the victory Morgan Freeman provides the voice-over reading Henley's poem.

The powerful message in Henley's poem is that we can be held prisoners of the past and be bound by the things which have happened to us; or we can release ourselves from captivity and live the life that we really want. Undoubtedly, there are terrible things which happen to people physically and mentally through accidents, natural disasters, other people's behaviour, and so forth. They can have a devastating effect on people's morale and confidence and this stress can seriously impact on their health leading to a downward spiral with health conditions adding to the impact of the sad and distressing memories of what happened.

It is natural and healthy to grieve about some things which have happened. This is nature's way of saying: "Slow down, take time to recover, and don't place yourself in new dangers when you are not fit to handle them." The Victorians held that when a loved one died people should mourn for a year before fully re-entering social events. This is about the time which it takes many people to recover from serious setbacks but this varies with some taking a shorter time and others needing a longer time to regain a positive zest for life.

The danger lies in those people who, almost exclusively, start to define themselves by the sad events which have happened to them. Instead of saying: "I am a person who has experienced happy and sad things in my life," they say: "This is what happened to me, it is who I am." They have adopted a victim mentality and cannot or will not try to find an alternative and more positive way of living. Everyone faces adversity in their lives and it is within our power to choose whether or not we wish to be constrained by these events. Should we blight the rest of our lives

167

because of a misfortune which befell us? Or should we take control of our future and lift ourselves up through hope in the future?

BROKEN DREAMS

We all have dreams but sometimes bad luck or fate intervenes to deprive us of achieving what we want. These setbacks can be devastating and some people never recover, but most find new dreams which can guide them and provide new purpose and direction. Picking ourselves up after a fall can be hard work but it is the only way forward and there are many examples which can provide us with role models.

Brian Clough was the sixth of nine children living in the unfashionable town of Middlesbrough. He became head boy at school but largely neglected his studies to play sport. Eventually, he was picked by his local soccer team, Middlesbrough FC, and went on to become their top scorer with 197 goals in 213 matches. He then moved to Sunderland FC and scored 54 goals in 61 games giving him the all-time highest ratio of goals per game in the English leagues. His success resulted in him playing for the national team.

Unfortunately, in one game he received a bad knee injury when he collided with the opposing team's goalkeeper. Two years onwards he returned but only played three games before retiring. The injury at the age of 27 and at the height of his skills was devastating.

For many people that would have been the end of their involvement with soccer and they would have found regular jobs. But Brian Clough picked himself up and, with his assistant Peter Taylor, went on to successfully manage a number of clubs. In particular they led Derby County to win the club's first English League Championship but, after falling out with the club's chairman, they joined Nottingham Forest.

This proved to be the most successful period in Forest's long history. When Clough and Taylor joined, the club was in the Second Division but the following season it was promoted to the First Division and finished third. The next season they won the League Championship which gave entry into the European Championship. Remarkably, they won the European Cup twice which was a stunning success for a relatively small club.

Clough's personality and success established such a connection with soccer supporters up and down the country that when he died they wanted to commemorate his achievements. Remarkably, three statues were erected, a number of books written and even a film illustrated his career. His undiminished love and appreciation of his hometown of Middlesbrough was commemorated by a statue depicting him walking from his home to the soccer ground.

RAIN CLOUDS CAN HAVE A SILVER LINING

We can often struggle with making the big decisions in our lives. Which way should we go? Which option should we take? It is not easy because we are very aware of the importance of making the right choice since it will have a major influence on our future.

On the other hand, we have little difficulty in making the minor decisions in our lives and often give them little thought. Life is too short to spend our lives in doubt and indecision with the small and routine choices. Yet, it sometimes happens that apparently small incidents can have massive impacts on our lives.

Take the case of Gareth Bull, a builder, who was on his way to a construction site when it started to rain. Because of the bad weather he was unable to work and so, to kill time until the rain stopped, he called into a shop where he bought a Euro-lottery ticket. His nine-year old son was always telling him that he was wasting his money but Gareth ignored this advice.

The next morning he checked his ticket and discovered that he was the only person to get all the numbers correct. He wandered dazed into the bedroom to tell his wife Catherine, who thought he was just joking. But they checked again and discovered that they had won over £40million ($63million). They plan to keep their 'dream' home which Gareth built and stay in their jobs. Their lives may have changed but they are keeping their feet on the ground. It is also possible that Gareth and Catherine's son may have changed his mind about the value of buying lottery tickets.

The reality is that sometimes big opportunities lie very close and we just need the hand of fate to bring them to us. There are major crossroads in our lives every day whether or not we are aware of them.

KEEPING THE DREAMS ALIVE

Our dreams are highly motivating and they make us get out of bed in the morning and also persevere when it would be much easier to just give up. Dreams give us goals and objectives which provide meaning and purpose to our lives as well.

If you ever speak with people who are despondent you will often find that they have few constructive thoughts about the future and about what they want to achieve. Instead, they often feel that they have reached a roadblock which is preventing them from moving forward. But it is important to have dreams and look forward, as Henry David Thoreau the US author and philosopher said:

"Do not lose hold of your dreams or aspirations. For if you do, you may still exist but you have ceased to live."

Yet, even in adversity it is possible to glimpse a faint light even if it does appear far away down the tunnel. There are countless people who have suffered appalling circumstances and have survived by giving themselves small positive things to think about, for example, people who have been imprisoned such as Viktor Frankl who survived the concentration camps, and Nelson Mandela who made plans for the future on Robben Island. Other people in difficult circumstances try to be positive because they know it will make them feel mentally better which will also have an impact on their physical condition. They also know that this makes the people around them feel better as well.

Where people are glum it often helps to have small enjoyable things to look forward to. These give us hope and a more positive outlook on life. Keeping our dreams alive no matter how large or small gives us life and energises us. Dreams give a focus and make us feel younger. As the author C. S. Lewis explained:

"You are never too old to set another goal or to dream a new dream."

ENVIRONMENT

We saw in Chapter 4 that young children who were able to resist the temptation of immediately eating a marshmallow were rewarded for their patience by receiving an extra one. This ability to defer gratification also led to them being more successful in their lives. The ability to take the long view into the future is an important one which also translates into making sure that the environment is preserved for future generations.

There is a strong temptation to let tomorrow take care of itself but if this involves the destruction of the natural environment then troubles may be stored up and increased in the future. Activity today should always take into consideration what it might mean tomorrow and one of the best ways to identify the consequences is through imagination.

By looking to the past we can learn lessons which help us make decisions today and which will influence the future. For example, there are numerous animals which have become extinct as a result of human action including the Tasmanian tiger and the North African elephant. There are also birds which have become extinct including the dodo and there are many others which are close to extinction. One of these is the New Zealand kakapo, a flightless ground living parrot, which is active at night to protect itself. However, early explorers introduced cats and stoats which resulted in a collapse in kakapo numbers and now only a few survive on remote islands. Department of Conservation staff are slowly but successfully encouraging the expansion of this unusual and very popular bird. Looking to the future can help us make important decisions about actions and behaviour which will influence not only our future but that of future generations.

AMBITION: VISUALIZE TO REALISE

"Ah, but a man's reach should exceed his grasp, or what's a heaven for?"
ROBERT BROWNING (1812 – 1889) SCOTTISH POET

Do you have a particular ambition which you wish to achieve? If so, you are not alone in seeking to change your current circumstances since almost everyone seeks to improve things – it is part of the human condition. This drive, this ambition, is what has enabled humankind to scale the highest mountains, walk on the moon, and seek cures for medical conditions and diseases.

And ambitions don't have to be stratospheric, they can be relatively ordinary: "I'm going to go to college or university." "I'm going to be an auto-mechanic." "I am going to have a nice comfortable house." "I'm going to be an artist, actor etc." If we set our minds to doing something we are already on our way to achieving it.

But the opposite perspective is also true. If we say: "I'll never achieve much in life." "I won't apply for that job because there are too many people applying." "No one will ever like me." Then, we will never pass the starting line and because of the self-fulfilling prophecy we will probably be successful – at achieving nothing!

You may have met people like those described above. Their ambitions drive them forwards and, although you may have your doubts about their potential to succeed, they can surprise you by reaching their objectives. Those people you have met who have no expectations or even negative ones also frequently find that they achieve what they expected. The extent to which we are successful often depends on our attitude; as Henry Ford said:

"If you think that you can or think that you can't, you are probably right."

BELIEVE IN YOURSELF

BELIEVE

For something to happen we must possess the belief that we can achieve our dreams. If there is too much doubt then we have already lost the battle and we will not even set out on the road to achieve our dreams. Eliminating ourselves from opportunities means that we have lost even before we have begun. The chances of winning the lottery jackpot may be quite small but if we don't buy a ticket there is absolutely no chance that we will win and change our lives forever. We have to enter the race to stand a chance of being successful.

Sometimes opportunities will drop into our laps if we are just present. Attending a meeting when we have other more pressing things to do means that being there gives us the opportunity to take part in the decisions which are being made and allows us to become involved. Staying elsewhere will mean that we will not be involved with projects etc. As Woody Allen, the actor and film director said:

"80 per cent of success is just showing up."

There are also some people who avoid the big challenges and only choose the small easily achievable ones. There is no harm in this but it can mean that they do not achieve their true potential and therefore sell themselves short. It is generally wise to begin with achievable targets and in this way our confidence grows with each little success and we begin to raise our sights higher and higher. Children are good examples of this principle. Often, because they have little experience, they prefer to stay in safe reassuring situations, but this means that they will not explore and learn more. However, with some support and hand-holding they become more skilled and more confident in their abilities and learn to spread their wings.

We need to believe in our dreams enough to try and make them come alive. If we don't possess this belief and confidence that they will happen then it is unlikely that we will even try. A few years ago 16-year-old Jessica Watson became the youngest person to sail unassisted around the world. She spent seven months on her 34-foot pink yacht battling forty-foot high waves and coping with homesickness. After her arrival at the Sydney Harbour Bridge finish line the Australian Prime Minister said that she was, "Australia's newest hero." Watson quietly disagreed and told the welcoming crowd:

"I'm an ordinary girl who believed in her dream."

AWAY WITH THE FAIRIES

The Irish have an expression for those people who are prone to daydreaming – they say a person is: "Away with the fairies." It is a kind and gentle way of saying the person lives in a world populated by the 'little people' and which has little connection with reality.

Dreams should be based in reality otherwise their only benefit is to make us temporarily feel better while we are lost in our fantasy world. The power of a dream is only truly realised when it is taken from the abstract world to the physical world. And, the only way to find out if an idea 'has legs' is to try it for real. If it works then it is no longer a fantasy but a concrete reality.

It is important not to allow people to label you as being 'away with the fairies.' If this does happen it will reduce your chances of achieving your objectives because if the people around you don't believe in your dream they are less likely to support you in your endeavours.

The best way to make people believe in your dreams is to demonstrate that you are not lost in the clouds but can actually deliver concrete achievements. These do not need to be earth-shattering and can be quite small ones such as taking the first small steps on the journey.

Wallace Wattles (1860 – 1911) was a 'new thought' writer who wrote many articles on self-help as well as a book *The Science of Getting Rich*. He believed in the practice of creative visualisation in which he formed a mental picture of what he wanted to achieve and then set out to constructively deliver on that vision. He was a practical and grounded person who was not away with the fairies and he wrote:

> *"Mind, however, that you do not do this as a mere dreamer and castle builder. Hold to the FAITH that the imaginary is being realized and to your PURPOSE to realize it. Remember that it is faith and purpose in the use of the imagination which make the difference between the scientist and the dreamer."*

PERSEVERANCE AND OPTIMISM

Think of people you have known for a long time from school, college, university or perhaps work. What are they doing now and how successful or unsuccessful are they? Of course, success is not always about earning vast amounts of money, or climbing the greasy corporate pole; it can be about having a fulfilling job or a warm loving and stable family life. When you look back, what elements of their character did you remember most about them; were they hardworking, diligent, lazy, dependable, lacking in concentration, intelligent etc.? What elements of their characters do you think had an impact on their achievements in life?

It turns out that intelligence helps to some extent but what is more important for success is perseverance – sticking to the task and keeping going until it is achieved. Success is also related to the resilience of a person i.e. the ability to pick themself up after a fall and keep going.

To observers it may appear that the person has achieved their dreams without much effort but the reality is probably quite different. One of the main reasons people achieve their dreams is that they have clearly identified their objectives and then devoted their energies to reaching them. To achieve a goal requires that other tempting opportunities and distractions are ignored. Only the goal is important and this means that instead of diluting energy across a wide range of targets all energies are concentrated on reaching the dream.

There may be many people who had similar dreams to the successful person but for one reason or another they have fallen out of the race. Often the problem is that they had too many dreams and they also kept their options open for further possibilities. This constant lookout for further opportunities may mean that when another one appears they are then pulled in that direction. And then another opportunity comes along and they follow that. This constant alighting from one thing to another, like a butterfly, can be fun and entertaining but it does not achieve much progress.

To achieve a dream often requires that the person be single minded; but this does not mean ignoring the people around them, family, friends and co-workers. However, it does mean that they may need to sacrifice short-term satisfaction in order that longer term benefits are achieved.

The Victorians were very conscious of the virtues necessary for achievement in life and frequently adorned buildings with advice to the inhabitants and passers-by. Perseverance was a popular virtue as can be seen in this date stone.

DREAM SUMMARIES

Plan your life, without planning things just happen.

We can all mental time travel into the past and into the future.

Life is not all plain sailing, strong winds and adverse conditions can knock us off track unless we have clear objectives.

We must have faith in our abilities to reach our destination even if we cannot see the whole of our journey.

Sometimes dreams are shattered but this does not mean we should stop dreaming, instead we should identify new dreams and head in their direction.

We should be custodians of our natural environment so that it remains a reality for future generations.

Persevering even during difficult times is one of the strongest indicators of a person's success.

8
LIVE THE DREAM: DREAMS INTO ACTION

"I have more respect for the fellow with a single idea who gets there than for the fellow with a thousand ideas who does nothing."
THOMAS EDISON (1847 – 1931) INVENTOR

Go confidently in the direction of your dreams. Live the life you have imagined.
Henry David Thoreau (1817 – 1862) author, philosopher

INTRODUCTION

It is very easy to lose oneself in a fantasy dreamland where everything is perfect. Temporarily, this will make us feel good because the brain encourages the release of hormones which give us a sense of wellbeing. But fantasising and building castles in the air have only limited value unless we take the concrete steps to make them real.

Taking these steps requires us to change our behaviour but this is not easy as can be seen by the failure of so many New Year resolutions. One of the numerous reasons why people fail to achieve their dreams is that everyday demands take precedence – we have to make a living; we have to look after family; we have to study etc.

Another reason for not achieving a dream is that we procrastinate – we put things off and say, "I'll get round to it tomorrow or next week." We put the dream in a drawer and then forget about it. Unless the dream is visible to us every day then we will forget about it which is why a dream board or vision board is a good strategy because their images can inspire us to see what the future might hold. As Shakespeare said:

"Thoughts are but dreams till their effects are tried."

If we find that we are not making progress bringing our dreams to reality then we need to carefully analyse the factors which are holding us back. In this way we can regain focus and motivation and make the changes and sacrifices which are necessary to reach our goals.

And, when we reach our dream objectives we need to make sure that we luxuriate in the achievement. Some people dedicate themselves to reaching the mountain top only to find that the view was not as rewarding as they had previously thought. Sometimes making the journey is more satisfying then arriving.

The chapter ends with the advice to begin the journey to achieving your dream because once that happens, fate, luck and providence seem to align themselves with what you want to achieve.

LIVING THE DREAM OR DREAMING OF LIFE?

The 3rd/4th century B.C. Chinese philosopher Chuang-Chou (Zhuangzi) wrote:

"Once upon a time, I, Chuang Chou, dreamt I was a butterfly, fluttering hither and thither, a veritable butterfly, enjoying itself to the full of its bent, and not knowing it was Chuang Chou. Suddenly I awoke, and came to myself, the veritable Chuang Chou. Now I do not know whether it was then I dreamt I was a butterfly, or whether I am now a butterfly dreaming I am a man. Between me and the butterfly there must be a difference. This is an instance of transformation."

TRANSLATION BY JAMES LEGGE

CASTLES IN THE AIR

The expression, 'castles in the air' generally means someone's hopes or plans which have little chance of materialising because they lack proper foundations. People can often lose themselves in these fantasy castles and Henrik Ibsen, the Norwegian dramatist, said:

> *"Castles in the air: they are so easy to take refuge in. And so easy to build as well."*

But, as has been described many times in this book, everything created by human beings once began with a dream. This is the starting point on which everything is constructed. And, since no idea arrives fully formed in our minds it takes time to analyse, build upon, subtract, alter and amend until the dream begins to look a realistic proposition.

Sharing our dreams with other people is another helpful means of testing how realistic they are. To do this we should put our thoughts into a logical and comprehensible shape which people can understand and enable them to provide valuable insights. If we are unable to clearly communicate our dream we should not blame others for pouring cold water on it.

Moreover, negative feedback may give a realistic assessment of the viability of a dream. Sometimes, the holder of the dream may not be grounded enough or may be too wrapped up in their ideas to see things clearly. Feedback should not be ignored since it might provide insights and help improve the prospect of success. As Henry David Thoreau explained:

> *"If you have built castles in the air, your work need not be lost; that is where they should be. Now put foundations under them."*

WHY PEOPLE DON'T ACHIEVE THEIR DREAMS

Many people set out on the road towards their dreams but not everyone arrives successfully. The reasons for this are numerous and include:

- It was only a fantasy which was good to think about but was never realistic and likely to be achieved.
- Other events intervened and life took a different route.
- There wasn't enough time to allocate to it.
- Making a living prevented embarking on the dream project.

- There was not enough deep commitment and motivation to achieve it.
- There was little, or no, support from family, friends or work colleagues.
- The person was not prepared to make sacrifices in other areas of their lives to achieve their dream.
- They didn't want to drop any of their many dreams and so diluted their efforts which resulted in none of them being achieved.
- They were always procrastinating and intending to do it 'tomorrow' which never came.
- They underestimated their dream.
- They were afraid of what they needed to do to achieve their dream.
- They were easily distracted and could never concentrate on doing what was necessary to achieve their dream.
- They gave up too easily.
- They lost sight of their dreams amid all the daily demands of life.
- They wanted to keep their options open so that they would not miss any other opportunities which might come along.
- They didn't link today's action with tomorrow's success.

All the reasons above are avoidable because they were self-created and the people had no one to blame except themselves. Sadly, the result of their failure to achieve their dreams can result in them feeling unhappy, stuck, and later in their lives regretting what they didn't achieve. People with a dream which they begin to put into action appear to have more direction, energy, and positive life-force. In the next section we will explore strategies to reach our dreams.

DREAM STRATEGIES

DECISION MAKING

People make decisions all the time e.g. whether or not to have a cup of tea or coffee, but it can be very hard to make decisions about areas which are much more important and perhaps represent a crossroads in our lives. Examples of these decisions include: choices about careers; relationships; taking a long-deserved holiday or saving the money for some other purpose; giving children more freedom to develop their independence or keeping a tighter rein until they are a little more sensible and mature etc. We weigh these decisions by projecting our minds forward to explore the possible outcomes of different courses of action.

On the other hand, many decisions are often made unconsciously without thinking about the decision making process. Yet, if we think about how we will approach a dilemma it is often possible to reach a more logical and sensible conclusion. There are a number of strategies which can help with this process:

- Be clear about an objective(s) and then prioritize the possible routes to the objective(s).
- Make a list of the pros and cons and see which has the most 'weight'.
- Ask advice from other people and carefully assess their suggestions.
- If it is difficult to choose between two options then they are probably evenly balanced and it may not matter which route is chosen.
- Flip a coin.
- Assess the financial cost of the options.
- Explore alternative options.

- Brainstorm very different possibilities – sometimes people become trapped in a certain way of thinking and cannot see alternatives.
- Does the decision need to be made now?
- Search for other guiding information before a decision is made.
- Do nothing – people avoid the decision and hope that circumstances will intervene and take the decision out of their hands.

ACHIEVING YOUR DREAM

Dreams are the starting point for everything people have created and if we wish to be successful then we should begin by writing them all down to make a dream list. These dreams can be in any area e.g. health, education, career, home, relationships, finance etc. and it doesn't matter how many there are or in what order. If the dreams are connected in some way then it can help to group them together.

The second stage is to give each a score out of ten for how desirable they are and then rank them in order from the most important down to the least important. This task may not be easy but it is very important to ensure that those at the top of the list merit their high ranking position.

The third stage is to take your top ranking dream and examine it carefully. Will it bring a significant change to your life; is it achievable; and, are you highly motivated and prepared to devote yourself to it? If your answer is 'No', then move onto the second choice dream and ask the same questions etc. Otherwise, stay with your number 1 dream which should be challenging but also have a realistic chance of success. All the other dreams should be placed safely in a drawer until you have achieved your top ranked dream. The reason for only focussing on one dream at a time is that aiming to achieve two or more will dilute your efforts and make it less likely that you will be successful in either of them. Of course, if they are small dreams from near the bottom of your list then it may be possible to squeeze an extra one into your schedule, but be careful, even small dreams demand time and energy.

All the elements which are required to successfully achieve the dream should be carefully identified, placed in sequential order and given a completion deadline. These elements, because they are smaller, will be more achievable and therefore when they are reached will encourage renewed motivation. Careful organisation and planning will provide a comprehensible overview and a route map which can be followed to the destination.

The next stage it to make your dream a part of your life so that it is with you all the time and becomes a habit. Changing your behaviour can be difficult but if you do it every day for at least a month it will then become routine and much easier. The more that it is in the forefront of your mind, the more opportunities you will encounter which will help progress on your journey.

Once the dream becomes part of your life many of the things which you encounter everyday should be assessed to see whether or not they will take you forward. For example, will it be better to go to that meeting or spend more time on something which will directly contribute to reaching the dream? Your dream is like a mission statement where you evaluate everything you do against whether or not it will help you achieve the mission. You should continually ask yourself, "Does this contribute to or hinder my progress to the dream?"

It is very important to discuss your dream with those who are close to you because most dreams require strong personal commitment and sacrifice which will impact on those around you. And, if you don't discuss it with them and get their support it will become very difficult, if not impossible to achieve. One very big advantage of proclaiming your dream is that this public commitment results in people asking you how you are progressing. This will keep you engaged so that you stay focussed on the objective. Another advantage of telling people about your dream is that they may be able to contribute and help you on your journey. If you do not tell people they will have no awareness or opportunity to contribute to pushing forward your dream.

Practise regular visualisation of your dream. To do this find a quiet place where you can sit and think without interruption. Next, begin visualising that you have successfully achieved your dream. What does it feel like; what can you see, what are the sounds; how are other people reacting to you? Do all of this in as minute detail as possible so that you believe that it is real. Then write all these details down and keep it in a place where you see it regularly so that it reminds you of the objective. If you practice this exercise several times a week it will begin to rewire your brain so that the dream becomes ever more real.

PLANNING YOUR FUTURE

One way to plan and organize how we will reach our dream future is to structure it in a simple way by breaking it up into discrete actions. For example, first I must do 'A' before I can do 'B', then 'C' and so on. Of course, it is also possible to conduct two or more actions simultaneously if they are not directly dependent on one another. In this way we can progressively make steps towards our goal.

Using a step by step approach involves a clear understanding of what we want to achieve. Although we have to physically begin with 'A', in reality we have to mentally work backwards from the end point putting in place each successive foundation i.e. to achieve the end objective 'Z.' we must ask, "What does 'Y' need to be." To reach 'Y', "What does 'X' need to be," and so on. Only then can we be clear about where we should begin.

This approach is often called 'backward-planning'. Once we have our steps clearly described and written down we can then begin the concrete

190

tasks which we have identified. We create our future by beginning from the future and thinking backwards

"Logic will get you from A. to B. Imagination will take you everywhere."
ALBERT EINSTEIN (1879-1955) THEORETICAL PHYSICIST

SETTING CLEAR TARGETS

Attempting to reach a dream can be like climbing Mount Everest and the fear which this causes has the potential to paralyse us into inaction. One practical way around this problem is to break the objective down into manageable sections which give us more confidence.

One example of breaking a giant objective into smaller achievable tasks is illustrated by climber Joe Simpson who, with his mountaineering partner Simon Yates, climbed the 6344m (20,814ft) Siula Grande peak in the Peruvian Andes. On the way down, Simpson fell and broke his leg and the only realistic way of getting down was for Yates to lower him down on a rope bit by bit. Inadvertently, Yates lowered Simpson over the edge of a cliff with a 30m plus drop below. Unfortunately Simpson could not climb back up the rope because of his broken leg and Yates could not move because he was holding the rope. Yates hung on to the rope for hours unable to communicate with Simpson and gradually became more and more exhausted. Eventually, realising that they both would die if he did not do something, he made the awful decision to cut the rope causing Simpson to crash into the crevasse below.

A distraught Yates then made his way down the mountain to their base camp believing that he had sent his mate to his death. Fortunately, a layer of ice had broken Simpson's fall and he eventually managed to crawl out of the crevasse but was then faced with a daunting journey down the mountain without food and water, and suffering from a broken leg and frostbite in his fingers.

Simpson quickly realised that he would be overwhelmed and give up if he tried to think about everything he needed to do to get down the mountain. Instead, he set himself small achievable targets such as reaching a specific rock in 20 minutes. Even though he was in great pain he forced himself to reach the rock, had a rest, and then set another target to reach. In this way he inched his way down the mountain and eventually shocked Yates who never thought he would see Simpson again.

Joe Simpson wrote a book about his adventure called, *Touching the Void* which was subsequently turned into an award winning film of the same name. Turning our dreams into small digestible chunks enable us to take the steps along the road and reach our destination.

APPRECIATE THE POSITIVE

There are occasions when people and organisations decide that where they are now is not satisfactory and look ahead to try and identify an alternative future. The danger of this negative focus is that they may then throw away all their good characteristics during the clear-out. Not surprisingly this can cause problems.

A more constructive way for people and organisations to change is to appreciate all their positive aspects and use these as a foundation to build towards the future. This approach is called appreciative inquiry and was developed by academic and author, David Cooperrider and colleagues. Appreciate inquiry has four main stages, sometimes called the four Ds: discovery, dream, design and destiny.

The first stage is Discovery which involves identifying all that is positive about ourselves or the organisation. Making a list of these good dimensions puts us in a constructive rather than destructive frame of mind and allows us to keep hold of them.

The second stage, Dream, involves challenging the current status quo, and generating positive images of what the future might hold. This can be done by using positive dialogue and self-talk which affirms present strengths and these can be used to create a better future.

The third stage, Design, builds an infrastructure and social organisation which will enable the 'dreamed' futures to be achieved. This might involve getting support from family and friends to allow you time to take a study course.

The final stage is Destiny or Delivery and involves carrying out the plans for the dream future. For example, this might involve taking a study course which will provide the foundation for career advancement or job change.

It is valuable and healthy to take a constructive perspective on the positive aspects of our lives particularly when we are dissatisfied with things. An appreciation of what we are doing well will often highlight the possible routes which we can take to our dream future.

POSTCARDS FROM THE FUTURE

'Postcards from the Future' is a visioning exercise in which a person imagines themselves in the future and they send a postcard back to themselves in the present day. In the postcard they describe in detail how things have changed from how they exist now.

Dear Me,

I arrived here in the future successfully. I have great work colleagues and my bosses really appreciate the way I am managing an important project. I have also met the most wonderful person and it looks promising.

You must come and visit.

Me
XXX

The detailed use of imagination can be a powerful way of building momentum and confidence within ourselves to change. If we can envision how things might be these pictures will attract us to change our behaviour in order to achieve our dreams. And, the more we practise imagining ourselves in the future the more we rearrange and strengthen the connections in the brain thus increasing the chances of us reaching our objectives.

Although, this exercise is called 'Postcard from the Future' it could be a letter or any other form of correspondence from your future self. This exercise is a simple one, just sit down and think deeply about the kind of you and type of world you wish to see at some time in the future. The distance to this future point in time will depend on your dreams and how long you think they will take to achieve e.g. if you are single and wish to have a settled family life with children you might be looking five or more years ahead; if you are considering a new job this might be anything from six months onwards.

"You are today where the thoughts of yesterday have brought you and you will be tomorrow where the thoughts of today take you."
BLAISE PASCAL (1623 – 1662) FRENCH MATHEMATICIAN AND WRITER

CREATING A DREAM BOARD OR VISION BOARD

A dream board or vision board is a way to help you create the life you want. This involves gathering a collection of pictures, texts and objects which have a powerful meaning for you and tell the story of what you want to be. They should be displayed somewhere that you will see numerous times each day and by doing so they will deeply imprint themselves in your brain and so encourage you to strive after your dreams and visions.

There are many ways to create a dream board. One way is to buy one and then personalize it with pictures, cuttings from magazines etc. Another

"Your Wish is My Command"

FOCUS on what you want and you WILL attract

ALL power is from within

COSTA BLANCA

We are what we think

1947   The era of the "New Look"

1. ASK
(Write it down, think it)

2. ANSWER
(Let the Universe respond)

3. RECEIVE
(Bring yourself in to alignment to receive)

Positive Energy draws positive things

What do you really want?

196

way is to put images on your computer or other devices and if you make t a screen-saver you will often see your dream future. Some people use a pin-board to present the images which mean a lot to them.

A popular place for a dream board is the refrigerator door. By using tape or magnets we can display the pictures and texts; move them around; change and replace them; and have a great deal of flexibility. We also visit the refrigerator regularly and therefore we are influenced by the images even when we may not be paying too much attention to them. Other places to locate a dream board include the office, bedroom or anywhere we visit frequently.

t is important that we take time each day to carefully look at our dream board. It is very easy to become so used to its presence that we don't notice that it is there. If you find that it no longer inspires you replace some of the pictures or consider whether or not your dreams have changed. The idea behind a dream board is that influences us and encourages us to search for and achieve our dreams.

'LL BE HAPPY WHEN I ACHIEVE MY DREAM

We spend about one-third of our waking lives thinking and dreaming about what we will do in the future and, when we concentrate on positive images, this can give us a feeling of well-being. Indeed, it is often the journey rather than the arrival which can provide the most satisfaction, or example, the Harvard University teacher, Tal Ben-Shahar described a similar experience when he was sixteen and won a national squash championship. After making many sacrifices and devoting himself to reach this objective he felt flat and didn't get the emotional satisfaction which he expected. Similarly, the golfer David Duval, recounted:

> "All my life I dreamt of winning something like an Open. Then when I got there I found myself asking 'Is that it?' Maybe I just enjoyed the journey more than the destination."

What can happen is that we set ourselves a target e.g. high grades, a prestigious job, a comfortable house, a partner etc. and promise ourselves that we will be happy when we reach that objective. However, when we arrive at that destination it can sometimes seem that the expectations do not match the reality. The phrase, "I'll be happy when..." is a common one which can sometimes distort our perception of happiness.

As we have seen, it is very important to think carefully about the future if we wish to make a success of our lives. However, one downside of thinking about the future too much is that we can spend all our time living in our dream world and fail to live in the present. After all, the only concrete thing we possess is the present, not the past nor the future! And it is only in the present that we can feel happiness and satisfaction. However, having a dream objective gives life meaning for many people and Albert Einstein advised:

"If you want to live a happy life, tie it to a goal, not to people or objects."

A Dream

In visions of the dark night
I have dreamed of joy departed –
But a waking dream of life and light
Hath left me broken-hearted.

Ah! what is not a dream by day
To him whose eyes are cast
On things around him with a ray
Turned back upon the past?

That holy dream – that holy dream,
While all the world were chiding,
Hath cheered me as a lovely beam
A lonely spirit guiding.

What though that light, thro' storm and night,
So trembled from afar –
What could there be more purely bright
In Truth's day-star?

EDGAR ALLAN POE

VISUALIZE TO REALISE

VISUALIZATION – CREATE THE PICTURE

To recap from Chapter 1, when we think about doing something we activate the same areas of the brain as if we are physically doing it. And as we know, if we regularly rehearse something physical e.g. a tennis serve, a speech, cooking a meal etc. we get physically stronger and increase our ability to do that activity. Similarly, mentally rehearsing an activity will strengthen the connections in our brains speeding up their operations, making our responses more automatic, and making our actions more natural and fluent.

We also saw in Chapter 1 that mental rehearsal of piano finger exercises and juggling caused the specific areas of the brain associated with these activities to grow. Likewise, taxi drivers who learned the 25,000 streets and 20,000 landmarks across London for *The Knowledge* examination had larger areas of the brain associated with spatial orientation than ordinary people. In addition, more experienced taxi drivers possessed larger areas of their brains devoted to spatial orientation than their less experienced colleagues.

More astonishingly, mental rehearsal alone can increase our physical strength, for example, repeatedly imagining we are lifting a weight with our finger. Sitting in an armchair and mentally rehearsing an activity again and again will enable us grow not just our mental strength but also our physical strength! Of course, thinking alone will not make us world champions it must be combined with dedicated and focused physical effort. But combining mental rehearsal and physical practice may produce an unbeatable performance.

Importantly, we also learned that we are not our thoughts since we can monitor what we are thinking about and decide whether or not we wish to concentrate on those things. Also, our thoughts influence our

feelings and therefore if we wish to change our feelings we also need to change what we are thinking about. If we wish to feel happy we need to have happy thoughts etc.

It would appear that our brains spend much of our waking lives thinking about what we are going to do in the future. They are designed to dream and that is what many visualisation exercises are about. There are some people who think that they are unable to visualize but this is not the case. If they can imagine the colour of their front door, or the face of a person they know etc. they have the ability to visualize. Visualisation is just remembering or imagining in a concentrated form.

To visualize effectively there are a number of key principles to follow such as using all our senses:

• It is important to create a picture in your mind's eye of what you want and the more intense the colours, the more active the picture the greater the likelihood that you will achieve it. The more attractive and alluring the picture increases the possibility that you will find a route to achieve what it is that you want.

• What are the sounds that you can hear as you undertake the activity? Is it the praise of your family, friends, the crowd etc? Perhaps it is the sound of nature such as waves lapping on the shore; the wind in the tree tops; the sound of birds or animals calling etc.

• Are there any smells which you associate with the activity such as the smells of floor polish, sea water, cut grass, exhaust gas etc.? When motorsport drivers are racing their senses are highly in tune with everything around them. For example, the three-time winner of the Formula 1 championship, Jackie Stewart, described how his main memory of one race was the smell of cut grass as the car in front clipped the grass verge.

• Are there specific tastes which you associate with the activity? Many chefs will not be able to describe the exact taste they are searching for but by sampling the sauce they are making they will be able to add specific ingredients to perfect the taste they want.

• What are the physical sensations when you are involved with the endeavour? How do your clothes, shoes feel? How do the physical objects or people you come into contact feel? Are they rough, smooth; round, angular, warm, cold etc.? Can you feel the warm sand under your feet or the waves as they caress your toes?

By using all our senses to imagine the future situation we can increase and strengthen the brain's connections. And, the more mental connections there are and the stronger they are, will increase our ability to create that perfect performance. People may have a preferred sense which they like to use, which is fine, but if that can be built on through the use of other senses then the experience becomes more intense.

In addition to using all our senses it is important to define our target. If we don't know where our target is then we will not be able to close in on it. And, if we keep our dreams vague and lacking in clarity there is a much smaller chance that we will achieve our objectives.

Sometimes, there is a temptation to keep our dreams imprecise so that we give ourselves flexibility to take other options as they come along. But this approach can result in us being pulled one way and then another as various opportunities tease and torment us. If we have carefully assessed and selected our objective then we should put all our energies into reaching it. Once it is achieved, we can then begin to follow the next dream.

Generally, it is best to begin practising visualisation techniques where we have peace and quiet so that we are not disturbed. Sitting or lying down, possibly with gentle music playing, will also aid our ability to visualize and encourage calm concentration. Gradually, our ability to visualize will grow stronger and stronger until we can do it in crowded places with lots of noise and distractions. Our focus will be on the visualisation and not on the other things happening around us. It is often possible to see this process in action among athletes waiting to begin a race – they appear to be in a world of their own and what they are doing is imagining the perfect state and the perfect race.

Use visualisation to experience a perfect performance whether it is a sporting event, musical performance, a presentation, meeting that dream person etc. If you can already draw upon previous positive experiences use these to help you construct that faultless activity. Sometimes, you might want to stitch together different elements from different positive experiences and build these up into the textbook perfect performance.

Be careful, when you are looking back at less successful experiences. When something does not go well you may revisit it to try and learn what went wrong so that you don't do it again. Re-evaluating an experience a few times is a natural thing to do; however, excessively and obsessively examining a failure will only cement that experience so deeply in your brain that you will find it hard to imagine doing it correctly.

To counteract these negative mental processes we need to build stronger mental pathways in which we perfectly execute the action. To do this we need to repeatedly mentally and physically rehearse perfect performances. The more you think positively, the less you will dwell on possible negative outcomes with the result that pessimistic mental pathways become weaker and your brain will default to the positive mental pathways. If the mentally correct way of doing something is stronger than the incorrect one the former will dominate and you will have a greater chance of success.

SPORTING DREAMS

*"Champions aren't made in the gyms. Champions are made from
something they have deep inside them – a desire, a dream,
a vision."*
MUHAMMED ALI, BOXER

The majority of ordinary people who take part in sport do so because
of the benefits which it gives them including greater fitness, health,
friendship and sense of well-being. There are also a group of people
who wish to perform at a high level and to do so they need to devote
themselves to their task pretty much all of the time.

Many sports coaches will describe how they have coached talented
people but the ones that were successful were the ones that were
dedicated. They committed themselves all the time and were not
discouraged by setbacks such as failures or injuries. What kept them
going through all the demanding training, and especially when
progress seemed to be going backwards, was the dream and the vision
of winning.

Most sportspeople use visualisation to help them prepare for and
achieve peak performance. And visualisation, or mental rehearsal, can
be undertaken in two main ways. The first is to imagine seeing yourself
running the race i.e. looking at yourself running from the outside like a
movie film. This is sometimes called dissociating. A more effective way
of visualising is to see everything directly through your own eyes as if
you were actually in the race. This is sometimes called associating. This
mental rehearsal can be further enhanced by imagining the sounds,
perhaps the starter's gun, the sound of the crowd etc.; and the feel of
your body as your legs and arms drive you forwards.

The more sensations you are able to imagine the more intense the
experience. In this way, the mind and body become more in tune with
one another and the stronger the connections become. And, as we have

seen, the more we mentally rehearse the stronger the brain connections become making it easier and increasing our chances of success. Of course we do not have to be a sportsperson to practice these mental techniques, they can be used by everyone to help dream and we can use them to help dream our futures.

DREAMS INTO ACTION

Dreaming is a fabulous way of increasing our motivation, exploring possible pathways, tuning our minds into recognising opportunities and increasing our luck. However, it is almost impossible to mentally explore all the possible outcomes and combinations which might happen.

It is only when we start to do something that other things begin to happen. For example, if we don't tell people that we are going to do something they will not have the opportunity to say: "I know a person who can help you with that." Or you might start a business and suddenly people approach you with further ideas and business opportunities. Our actions do not happen in a vacuum and as soon as we start to say or do something this impacts all around us.

Sometimes people are held back from taking action because they want everything to be perfectly right before they begin. This is understandable but it can also prevent them from achieving their dreams. While you are planning the perfect strategy someone else may jump in with less preparation but nevertheless achieve success. This can often happen in business where a person is organising their plans and someone else sets up and steals the market opportunity. Similarly, in our personal lives, waiting for the perfect moment to ask someone on a date might never happen and another suitor grabs a limited opportunity.

Dreams are the starting point for us. We must then put them into action to prevent them becoming just fantasy. As soon as we set out on the road we encounter new possibilities which we would never have seen or experienced sitting at our desk. This perspective was beautifully described in 1951 by William Murray, the leader of a Scottish climbing expedition to the Himalayan mountains. In his book he explained how there had been a lot of talk but little action and then they bought their tickets for the boat to Bombay. Suddenly, things started to happen and fortune smiled by helping the expedition in numerous ways which would never have happened had they not taken that first step. Murray exclaimed:

"Until one is committed, there is hesitancy, the chance to draw back. Concerning all acts of initiative (and creation), there is one elementary truth, the ignorance of which kills countless ideas and splendid plans: that the moment one definitely commits oneself, then Providence moves too. All sorts of things occur to help one that would never otherwise have occurred. A whole stream of events issues from the decision, raising in one's favour all manner of unforeseen incidents and meetings and material assistance, which no man could have dreamed would have come his way. I have learned a deep respect for one of Goethe's couplets: 'Whatever you can do, or dream you can do, begin it. Boldness has genius, power, and magic in it'."

DREAM SUMMARIES

Building castles in the air is the starting point for all endeavours, however, foundation must also be added if we are to achieve our dreams.

People don't achieve their dreams for many reasons including: distractions, lack of commitment, procrastination, daily demands of life, and having too many dreams.

Decide on one dream only and then devote all your energies to achieving it.

Plan your future by working backwards from your final endpoint.

Don't attempt to climb the mountain in one go. Set yourself small achievable targets and build your confidence when you succeed in reaching them.

When changing your life, don't throw away all your good attributes along with the negative ones. Appreciate what you are good at.

Send yourself a postcard from the future describing in desirable detail what it is like.

Create a dream board or vision board which has pictures, words and other things which present your future life.

Remember to enjoy your life in the present – it is all you have.

Create an intense vision of what your future life will be like through visualization.

Go out and make it happen: "Whatever you can do, or dream you can do, begin it. Boldness has genius, power, and magic in it."

SELECT BIBLIOGRAPHY

Backley, S. and Stafford, I. (2000) *The Winning Mind: A Guide to Achieving Success and Overcoming Failure*, London, Aurum Press.

Bauby, J-D. (2008) *The Diving Bell and the Butterfly* (Le scaphandre et le papillon), London, Harper Perennial.

Ben-Shahar, T. (2007) *Happier: learn the secrets to daily joy and lasting fulfilment*, New York, McGraw-Hill.

Chabris, C. and Simons, D. (2010) *The Invisible Gorilla: And the other ways our intuitions deceive us*, New York, Crown Archetype, Random House.

Cooperrider, D. and Whitney, D. *Appreciative Inquiry: A positive revolution in change*, San Francisco, CA, Berrett-Koehler.

Frankl, V. E. (2004) *Man's Search for Meaning: The Classic Tribute to Hope from the Holocaust*, London, Rider.

Freud, S. (1913) *The Interpretation of Dreams*, New York, The Macmillan Company.

Gallwey, W. T. (1986) *The Inner Game of Tennis*, London, Pan Books.

Kampusch, N. (2010) *3096 Days*, London, Penguin.

Murray, W. H. (1951) *The Scottish Himalayan Expedition*, London, J. M Dent and Sons Ltd.

Parton, D. (2012) – http://www.imaginationlibrary.com/ [accessed 03/04/2012]

Plensa, J. (2012) http://www.dreamsthelens.com/ accessed 03/04/2012.

Robertson, I. (1999) *Mind Sculpture: Unleashing your Brain's Potential*, London, Bantam Books.

Seligman, M. (1998) *Learned Optimism: How to Change Your Mind and Your Life*, New York, Free Press.

Simpson, J. (1998) *Touching the Void*, London, Vintage Books.

Smit, T (2002) *Eden*, London, Corgi.

Wilkinson, J. (2009) *Tackling Life*, London, Headline.

Wiseman, R. (2003) *The Luck Factor*, London, Century.

Dream: Your Life, Your Future